KV-011-964

JOHN HUME

PERSONAL VIEWS

This book is dedicated to the tenacity
of the S.D.L.P.'s membership and
the memory of deceased colleagues.
Their sense of purpose and resolve
in standing up for peace and reconciliation
in spite of all the pressures and provocations
has given inspiration and strength.
It is a source of both pride and
humility to lead such leaders.

JOHN HUME
PERSONAL VIEWS

Politics, Peace and Reconciliation in Ireland

Foreword by
Senator Edward M. Kennedy

Introduction by
Douglas Gageby

Edited by
Jack Van Zandt and Tom McEnery

ROBERTS RINEHART PUBLISHERS

Published in Ireland by
Town House and Country House, Trinity House, Ranelagh, Dublin 6

ISBN 1–86059–023–3 Hardback

ISBN 1–86059–024–1 Paperback

A catalogue record for this book is available from the British Library

Published in England, Scotland and Wales by
Roberts Rinehart Publishers, c/o Airlift Book Company,
8 The Arena, Mollison Avenue, Enfield, Middlesex EN3 7NJ

ISBN 1–57098–110–8

The moral authority of the author has been asserted.

Text © 1996 John Hume
Foreword © 1996 Senator Edward M. Kennedy
Introduction © 1996 Douglas Gageby

Tom McEnery was the mayor of San Jose, California, from 1983 to 1990. He received a master's degree in Anglo-Irish history from Santa Clara University where he wrote his dissertation on Michael Collins and the evolution of Irish nationalism. He is the author of several works, including *The New City State* (Roberts Rinehart, 1995), and is a long-time friend of John Hume.

Jacket design: Wendy Williams

Typesetting: Red Barn Publishing, Skeagh, Skibbereen, Co. Cork

Printed in Ireland by ColourBooks, Dublin

Contents

Part Four: Ireland at Peace

Part Five: A New Ireland

Afterword

Foreword

I first met John Hume in 1972. At the beginning of that year, British troops had shot and killed thirteen unarmed civilians in John's hometown of Derry—a day that became known as Bloody Sunday—and the conflict in Northern Ireland was boiling over. I had long known of John's leadership of the civil rights movement there and I called him that fall and asked if he could meet me. Shortly afterwards we had dinner together and I heard of his hopes and dreams for his people and for Ireland.

Ever since that evening I have had enormous respect for John, his courage and his leadership. He has had a profound influence on my thinking and on the attitudes of Congress and the American Government towards the conflict; he has often been called the 101st Senator from Northern Ireland. Foremost in the Social Democratic and Labour Party for more than a quarter century, he has been and continues to be an eloquent and powerful voice for peace: advocating non-violence absolutely and a just settlement that respects the rights and aspirations of both communities. As John has so ably preached throughout his career, bombs and bullets are not the answer to the problems of Northern Ireland. The answer lies in the people of that special island themselves.

It is a most historic and hopeful time for Ireland. Many people deserve credit for the recent breakthroughs in the peace process in Northern Ireland. But few, if any, deserve greater credit for advancing the cause of peace than John Hume. President Kennedy would have called him a "Profile in Courage", and so do I.

Senator Edward M. Kennedy
Boston
January 1996

Ireland
Border
County boundaries
0 10 20 40 60 80
miles
Derry
Donegal
Derry
Antrim
Tyrone
Belfast
Fermanagh
Down
Leitrim
Armagh
Sligo
Monaghan
Cavan
Mayo
Roscommon
Louth
Longford
Meath
Westmeath
Galway
Dublin
Galway
Dublin
Offaly
Kildare
Leix
Wicklow
Clare
Carlow
Kilkenny
Limerick
Tipperary
Wexford
Waterford
Kerry
Cork
Cork

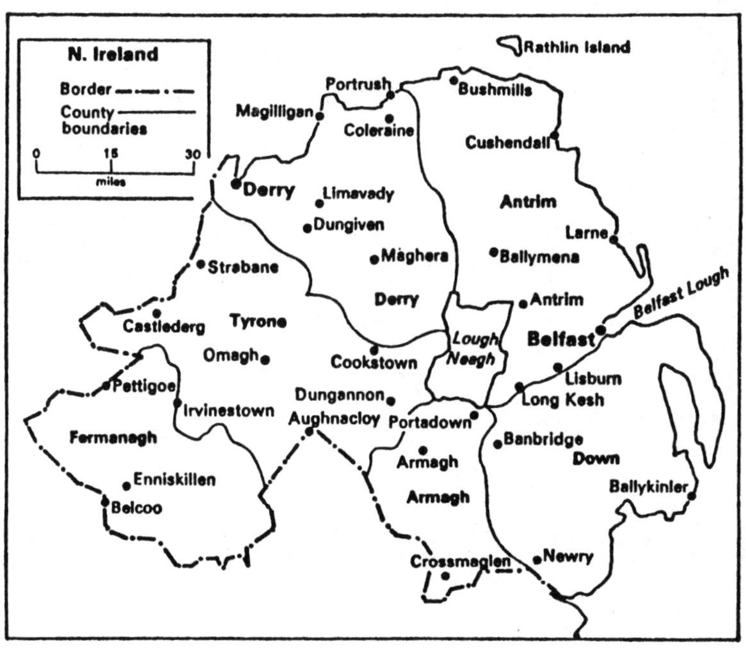

N. Ireland
Border
County boundaries
0
15
30
miles
Rathlin Island
Portrush
Bushmills
Magilligan
Coleraine
Cushendall
Derry
Limavady
Antrim
Dungiven
Larne
Strabane
Maghera
Ballymena
Derry
Antrim
Belfast Lough
Castlederg
Tyrone
Lough Neagh
Belfast
Omagh
Cookstown
Lisburn
Pettigoe
Long Kesh
Dungannon
Irvinestown
Aughnacloy
Portadown
Fermanagh
Banbridge
Armagh
Down
Enniskillen
Ballykinler
Armagh
Belcoo
Newry
Crossmaglen

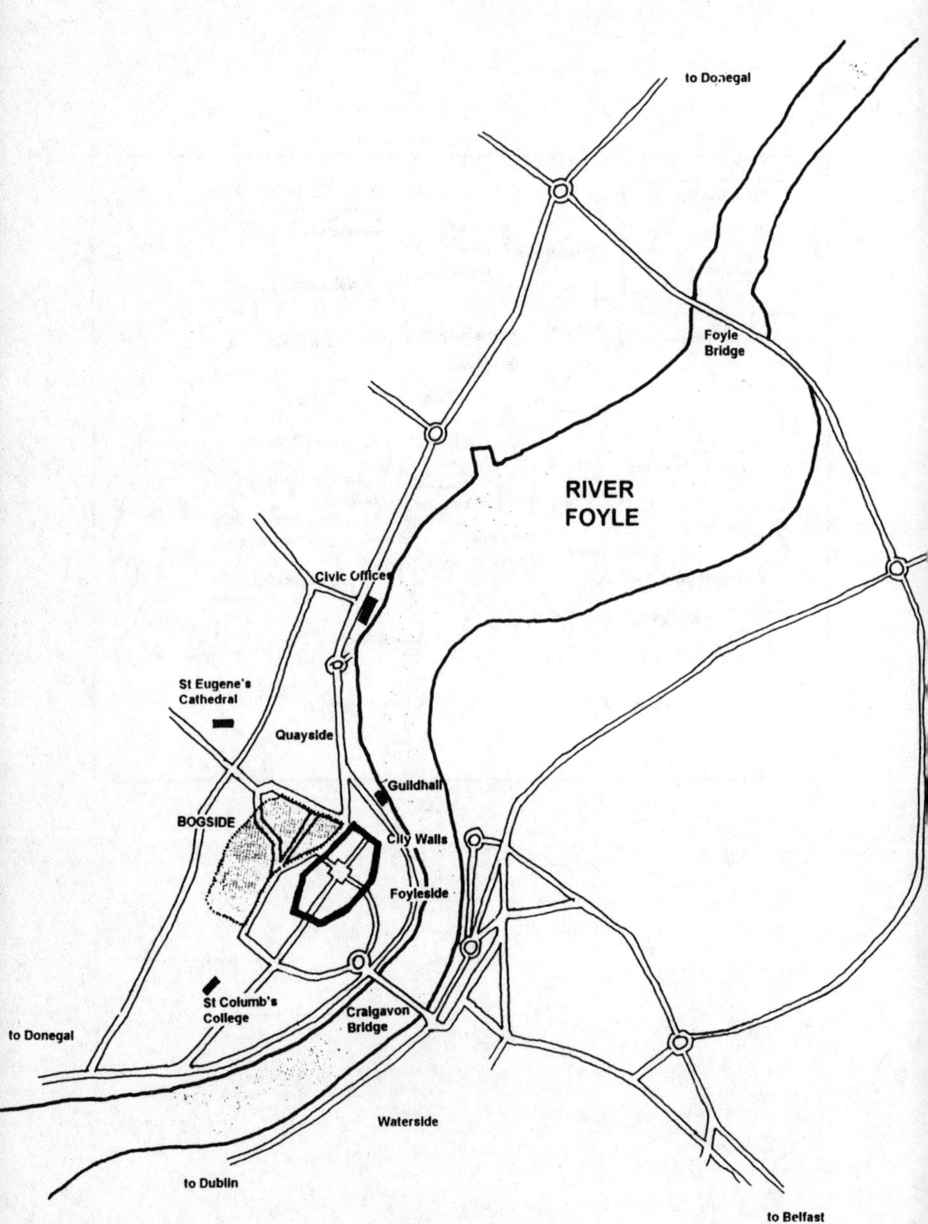
to Donegal
Foyle
Bridge
RIVER
FOYLE
Civic Offices
St Eugene's
Cathedral
Quayside
Guildhall
BOGSIDE
City Walls
Foyleside
St Columb's
College
Craigavon
Bridge
to Donegal
Waterside
to Dublin
to Belfast

D·E·R·R·Y

Introduction

The first chapter gives us the heart of the whole story and of the man. "I was anxious to give something back to the community." This in a street that was poverty-stricken, with high unemployment.

John had benefited from the free public education made available by the Education Act of 1947 and his first contribution to the community was to become involved in the Credit Union movement. And so it was that the Bogside had the first Credit Union in Northern Ireland—with £7 in savings and four members. Today the Derry Credit Union has 14,000 members and £21 million.

John is a doer as well as a thinker, active on behalf of the people: a servant of the people. And his passion for that unique city Derry is a sound foundation for his devotion to Ireland and Europe.

One-third of Derry's citizens ruled, through a system of gerrymandering, but John's response to such injustice was that mere complaining would get his people nowhere. "After all, weren't our heads and hands as good as theirs any day."

The founding of the Credit Union was his first important political step. The next was that the people should take control of providing their own housing, instead of asking the politicians to do it for them. So, in 1965, he and Father Anthony Mulvey set up the Derry Housing Association, with John as chairman. In the first year they housed 100 families; Derry Corporation housed none.

Hume was an activist, but he learned early that violence was no solution to the problems of Derry or Ireland. He quotes—particularly apt for Northern Ireland—Martin Luther King: "The old law of an eye for an eye leaves everybody blind." And, again so poignant in his home city and country: "If you use the methods of your oppressor, you will end up worse than your oppressor."

He was a leader in the civil rights movement of the late sixties. My wife Dorothy and I went up from Dublin to many of the marches. One time, the marchers crossed the bridge in Derry to be halted on the city side by the police. A young man at the front shouted back to the crowd, "Down everyone," and made downward gestures with his hands. "I'll go forward and talk to these people." We all sat down. So this young man, in a check jacket as I remember it, went forward to parley and eventually got us through. "That's John Hume," said people around us. It was November 1968, and the first time I had ever seen him.

We have met John and his wife Pat many many times since then, and learned that the often solemn-looking, eloquent man of public life is, after hours, so to speak, relaxed and good-humoured and even loves to sing a song. This used to be "Bunch of Thyme". The other day I asked him what his favourite party piece is now. "Oh, 'The Town I Love So Well'," he said, "Derry's national anthem. Written by a Derryman, Phil Coulter."

What Hume sees, and what not so many people in the north see, is that the siege mentality of the Unionists led to equally frozen attitudes on the Nationalist side. "Both behaved like threatened minorities and only by removing the fears which they both feel can a just and durable solution be found." The northern state, in other words, "served only to extend and aggravate this conflict by compressing the clash of majority and minority within an even more narrow and rigid territorial, economic and social confine".

John beat the then leader of the Nationalist Party, Eddie McAteer, whom he rightly describes as "an honourable and highly respected man", in the 1969 elections for the Stormont parliament. It was not that the old Nationalist Party, of which McAteer was a lively and personable leader, had been lacking in men of quality. Joe Devlin and T. J. Campbell are names that spring to mind, and above all Cahir Healy, who, twice interned, spoke words not dissimilar to those of Martin Luther King: "Victory is not with those who can inflict the most pain, but it is inevitably with those who suffer most."

But times had changed. Younger men with new ideas came on the scene. Soon these were to form the Social Democratic and Labour Party, with Gerry Fitt as the party's first leader and Hume as his deputy. They also included, among others, Ivan Cooper, Paddy Devlin, Paddy O'Hanlon and Austin Currie (Fitt and Devlin later withdrew). Today John's able deputy is Seamus Mallon.

This book brings you through the despair of the violence, the burning of Bombay Street, and on to the near miracle of the Power-Sharing Executive, where Unionists and SDLP, Protestants and Catholic Ministers seemed to be opening up a new era not only for the north of Ireland but for all Ireland. For the first time, the north had a mixed government. Further, the principle of a Council of Ireland was accepted. The north would continue to be a part of the United Kingdom.

This all happened under the Conservative government of Ted Heath. The Labour government which succeeded it surrendered, under threat from what Hume describes as a paramilitary minority on the Unionist side. The Ulster Workers' Council strike brought the north to a standstill, and the British government backed down. In Hume's opinion, to succeed against the strike the British government need not have used force. The vast majority of the people did not go on strike, but it was was most effective in the electricity services. However, Hume believed that the government should have been able to provide the essential services.

Unfortunately, the government's "political cowardice" was a disaster and the surrender, writes Hume, had long-lasting consequences, "because extreme unionism or loyalism was encouraged in its belief that it could henceforth resist and jettison any British policy for Northern Ireland which involved conceding power to the minority: 'The Orange Card'."

One of the passages in the book that could most be taken to heart in all parts of Ireland begins: "We all need a new and generous vision. We need both to abandon the sterile exclusivity of 'ourselves alone' and we need the positive encouragement of the third party—the British government." Hume invites Protestants "who have that wider vision to step forward and, by so doing, mount a positive challenge to those of my own tradition to meet the responsibilities we have not yet measured up to, to spell out in clear and tangible terms what we mean by unity, what we mean by partnership, what we mean by reconciliation".

John Hume knows that there is no instant solution to the "Irish question". He believes that the problem is not a territorial one. It is a question of people living with each other, no matter how great their diversity. Unity in diversity is the goal. But never through violence.

He writes: "No instant package will wipe away the damage done over the centuries. But I am absolutely certain that agreement will eventually emerge... The twenty-first century will be a post-nationalist and interdependent world. Through our own efforts and the support of our friends throughout the world, Catholic, Protestant and Dissenter will come together on our small island and at last the gun will have no role in the politics of our land."

John Hume must be our most travelled politician. London, Brussels, Strasbourg, Washington and New York are only the main routes which he tirelessly covers. But his own home town is among the most original of all. Paul of Tarsus said that he was a citizen of no mean city. Derry has many of the attributes of a City State. Its citizens, of both stripes, have more than a love for it: they have awe and respect, too.

When I went to school in Belfast, the headmaster of the Academy was Alec Foster, a Derryman. He was a classical scholar, but Derry was somehow brought into study and conversation with a relevance which was not always apparent to his pupils. He pronounced it "Durry", which is very close to the Irish *Doire*. Derry—there was no place like it. (And there was no such place as Londonderry in his canon.) We had Derry with everything. Derry was one of the great cities, to him, and to everyone—apparently—who was ever born there.

John Hume bears well the vituperation that has occasionally descended on him, especially when he decided to work with Gerry Adams of Sinn Féin to attempt to bring about a ceasefire. In public he often presents a solemn, if not lowering, countenance. His friends, however, are aware of his warmth and the special quality of the relationship between himself and his wife Pat.

Derry was, in the bad old days, a place of conflict. I remember Bernadette Devlin, at one of the civil rights marches, standing outside the Guildhall, and her voice rang off the old walls as she described Derry as "this capital city of injustice". It is no longer a city of injustice. It is bustling; it is smiling; it is an example to all the other cities of the west of Ireland, particularly on how to pull yourself up by your boot straps.

I remember, too, how in the late forties, as a reporter with the *Irish Press*, I was sent to Derry to take a look at conditions there. I arranged to see the mayor, Sir Basil MacFarland.

Sir Basil was an imposing man, as he sat at his desk. I think I had a word or two with him about a relation of my wife who had known him, and then I asked him my first question. It was roughly along the lines of "What are you doing to the Catholics here?"

Sir Basil rose slowly from his seat, pointed his finger at the door and said, "Out, Gageby. Out!" And out I went. I was strolling towards the river when I heard feet hurrying behind me. It was the smiling official who had ushered me into the mayor's office.

"Sir Basil would like you to come back. Mind you, you weren't very tactful, and he is a bit fiery. But he does want you to come back." Whatever Sir Basil said and whatever I wrote, I may one day dig out of the files.

Douglas Gageby
April 1996

Douglas Gageby is a former long-time editor and director of the *Irish Times.* He was the first editor of the *Evening Press* and, prior to that, editor-in-chief of the Irish News Agency.

He was born in Dublin in 1918, but his father, a civil servant, moved the family to his native city of Belfast in 1922.

He returned to Dublin in 1937, to study at Trinity College, and has lived there most of his life. In 1944 he married Dorothy Mary Lester, eldest daughter of Sean Lester, an Irish diplomat who was High Commissioner of Danzig for three years and subsequently the last Secretary-General of the League of Nations.

He is currently completing a memoir of his late father-in-law.

Vision is the art of seeing the invisible.

Jonathan Swift

Part One

Beginnings

— 1 —

Bogside Roots

And one read black where the other read white, his hope
The other man's damnation: Up the Rebels, to Hell with the Pope,
And God save—as you prefer—the King or Ireland.

Louis MacNeice

When I was growing up in Derry, my father, who was unemployed, used to say to me, "Stick to the books, son, it's the only way forward." He was right. What has transformed Derry over the last thirty or forty years is the introduction of public education for all. In particular it has transformed the Catholic community, the people who have suffered most from discrimination and unemployment.

I was born in Derry in 1937, the eldest of seven children. My roots lie deep in the Catholic area of Derry known as the Bogside. My maternal grandfather was a docker and my mother, Annie Doherty, was born and lived in an area now known as Free Derry Corner, a famous row of houses in the heart of the Bogside. Two of my aunts are still alive and continue to live there.

My father's grandfather, Willie Hume, was a stonemason who came from Scotland to build station houses for the new railway in Donegal, where he married my great-grandmother and settled during the second half of the nineteenth century.

My parents married when my father was forty-six and my mother was thirty-two. In the early years of World War II my father, who had fine handwriting, was employed in the Food

Office to write the names and addresses on the ration books. Later he changed jobs and worked in the Derry shipyards repairing ships. When the war ended, the shipyard closed and he, like many others, lost his job and remained unemployed for the rest of his life.

My father was a very special man. His formal education ended at primary school—I remember him telling me that he left school when he was twelve—yet he was a great reader, especially of westerns and detective stories, and he had exquisite copperplate handwriting. One of my earliest memories as a young boy is of sitting with him at the wooden table where our family ate our meals, I at one side doing my homework and he at the other writing letters to government departments for local people with little education who had housing, unemployment or other problems. From my earliest years, I was very conscious of the human effects of the serious social and economic problems of our city.

My mother was very intelligent but totally uneducated, as she had not had the chance to go to school. She could only write her own name. She, like many of the women of Derry, was a dominant influence in the family. Many women in the neighbourhood worked in the factories in the daytime and then worked at home at night. To make ends meet, my mother was an outworker for the shirtmaking industry. She worked as a patent turner, which meant that she prepared the shirt collars. She would wait until all my younger brothers and sisters had gone to bed before she started, and I would sit up late with her. I was her secretary; I counted the collars, tied them up and wrote down the number for her.

Grandmother Doherty was a great friend of mine—she always encouraged me with my schooling, and we were very fond of each other. Her house was nearer to my school than my own, so I went to her for lunch every schoolday. She was an excellent cook and while she prepared the meal I would run errands for her, such as buying her snuff, for which she had a great fondness.

Nobody then had cars so I walked to and from school with my friends, returning home after school to play in the street, games of our own creating. I feel very fortunate to have grown up in an area with such a strong sense of community and neighbourliness and concern for other people.

As far back as I can remember I was always aware of discrimination against the Catholic community. Yet, despite this, the streets near us where we lived in the Glen district, on the edge of town, were Protestant streets and we often played together. We played each others' games, and I even ended up being a senior cricket player. The common sense community in which I grew up was never anti-Protestant, but we were against the injustices being perpetrated by the politicians. However, at certain times of the year—during what was known as the "marching season"—the tensions would always surface.

Politics of any description were never discussed in our family—they were not part of our world. Because the politicians were of the generation that succeeded the creation of the "border" in Ireland, politics in Derry in those days was mainly about partition. It was felt, quite simply, that the border would not last, that eventually it would have to go. Nationalist politics was always emotional; elections were about flag-waving, and the real problems of unemployment, housing and poverty—the problems of politics except those of consequence of discrimination—were rarely an issue.

My father would have been oriented towards socialism, but there was really no effective Labour Party in his day. One of my earliest memories—and one that I have frequently quoted—is of going to an election meeting at the top of our street when I was about ten years old. It was a Nationalist meeting and they were all waving flags and stirring up emotions for a united Ireland and the end of partition. When my father saw that I was affected, he put his hand gently on my shoulder and said, "Son, don't get involved in that stuff," and I said, "Why not, Da?" He answered simply, "Because you can't eat a flag."

That was my first lesson in politics and it has stayed with me to this day. Politics is about the right to existence—the right to life—bread on your table and a roof over your head. It doesn't matter what flag you wrap around you when you stand in the dole queue or are forced to emigrate to another country to earn a living. A flag should symbolise the unity of the whole community. It should never be used as a party political or sectional emblem.

Despite growing up in an area of great poverty, I was one of the lucky ones who benefited from the introduction of free public education. At the age of ten, I passed what was called the Eleven-Plus examination. This enabled me to receive a government scholarship which paid my fees to attend St. Columb's College in Derry. Up until my generation, only the sons of business and professional people could afford to go to St. Columb's and consequently the school was very small. However, when the children of poor working-class families started to gain access to the school, it expanded very rapidly and huts had to be built to house extra classrooms.

On leaving school, I studied for three years to be a priest, but eventually decided to give it up. For my degree I studied French and History at Maynooth College in County Kildare. While at university, I spent my summers in France. I first visited St. Malo in Brittany in 1960 and then the following year I attended classes at the *Institut Catholique* in Paris where I learned to speak French fluently. Until this time I had never been out of Ireland, not even to visit England.

My European experience allowed me to study Irish history in an objective way and influenced my subsequent thinking very heavily. Once I was able to see the tradition of attitudes which prevailed in Ireland I could grasp the real nature of the problem, which eventually became my central political thesis.

After university and my studies in France, I came back to Derry an educated man and lived in our family's rented council house, which had two bedrooms and an outside toilet. My parents were still very poor, so, naturally, when I secured my first job as a teacher I would turn over my wages to my mother, and she would then give me back something from them for myself.

Our street was still poverty-stricken, with very high unemployment, and, as one of the lucky ones, I was anxious to be able to give something back to the community and do something about the problems of those who were less fortunate.

One of the first things I did after my return to Derry was to involve myself in the foundation of the Credit Union movement. We modelled this on information supplied to us by the enormously successful US Credit Unions. The Bogside in Derry had the first Credit Union in Northern Ireland, of which I was the treasurer, responsible for collecting the money on Friday nights and Saturday afternoons. My wife, Pat, is also from Derry and we were married in 1960, and every Sunday she would read out the Credit Union slips to me and I would fill in the ledgers.

We founded the Derry Credit Union on 30 October 1960 with four people and seven pounds. Today it has fourteen thousand members and twenty-one million pounds.

The people involved with me in founding the Credit Union—all voluntary work at that time—were young teachers like myself, clergy and members of the local community such as Paddy Doherty, Paddy Joe Doherty, Michael Canavan, Seamus Bonner, Dr. Jim Cosgrove, John Bradley and Father Anthony Mulvey. It was these same people who were later to encourage me to go into politics.

We were a very small group at the start, but we called public meetings and gradually persuaded people of the benefits of joining. Eventually, I would travel all over Northern Ireland and further, giving lectures on how Credit Unions worked and encouraging other communities to set them up.

By the time I was twenty-seven years old, I was president of the Credit Union movement throughout the whole of Ireland—the Credit Union League of Ireland—and international vice-president of the movement throughout the world. At my first international Credit Union meeting, in Dallas, Texas, in 1962, I met Senator, soon to be Vice President, Hubert Humphrey when he addressed the meeting. If I did nothing else in my life other than my involvement founding the Credit Unions, I would be a happy man.

Only a third of the population of Derry in the early 1960s was Protestant, but they were able to govern the city through a process of gerrymandering. This was achieved by dividing the city into three wards, and, since they controlled public housing, they were able to put all the Catholics into one ward and then give that ward just eight seats while the other two wards had six seats each. In this way, even though there were more Catholics in the city, the Protestants always won the elections by twelve seats to eight.

Nationalist politics at that time was understandably based in the negative—complaints about discrimination, about the shortage of housing, lack of jobs and the partition of Ireland. My response was to question the validity of always complaining and to encourage action—after all, weren't our heads and our hands as good as theirs any day, so why didn't we use them? The founding of the Credit Union provided, I felt, a shining example of what could be achieved by working together for ourselves. Self-help was the way forward.

The next step along the self-help road was our decision to attempt to build our own houses instead of asking the politicians to do it for us. So, in 1965, I helped to set up the Derry Housing Association, the founder of which was Father Anthony Mulvey. I became chairman, and we started the slow process of housing our own people. This was facilitated by having our office open during the week and inviting people to come in to discuss their problems.

The outcome was that, upon analysis of the situation, we found that there were three different kinds of housing problem. First, there were those people who could afford to buy their own house, but who did not know how to go about it. When buying a house, it was necessary to borrow from a building society, but first you had to have a deposit. So we organised methods by which these people could save in the bank for when they would need a deposit in order to buy their own house.

The second group of people were those who would have been able to afford to buy their own house but for the fact that their rent was so high, due to landlord exploitation of our housing problem, that they could not manage to save a deposit. In this instance, we took over some terraced buildings, turned them into apartments and let them out to people at double an economically reasonable rent. After two years, we gave them back half the rent as a deposit to buy a new house of their own.

The third group consisted of those who would never be able to afford to buy a house, and our solution here was to build good houses for them to rent at a fair rate. In the first year, in the mid-sixties, we housed one hundred families while in the same year the public housing authority, Derry Corporation (the city council), housed none. However, when we subsequently applied to build seven hundred more houses, the same corporation refused us permission. It was patently clear that our application was turned down because we were building the houses in the wrong area, thus upsetting the gerrymandered voting pattern. At this point, we decided that we had no choice but to voice our protest in terms of civil rights.

At that time, the two people who had an enormous influence on my thinking were John F. Kennedy and Martin Luther King. The people of Ireland took great pride in President Kennedy, and, having listened carefully to what he had to say, I found his words to be of supreme relevance to our own problems in Northern Ireland. Martin Luther King was of particular importance to me because of his campaign against discrimination. I still have two posters on the wall of my house, one of John F. Kennedy and his quotation, "One man can make a difference, but every man should try." The other is of Martin Luther King's "I had a dream" speech, which was given to me by his wife, in later years, in Atlanta.

I remember my shock when I heard, on the radio and the television, of the assassination of Martin Luther King. I was at home in my house in Derry, which in those days was a small bungalow above where I live now. Stunned, I wondered why, why would anybody do such a thing? I often use one of his quotes—"the old law of an eye for an eye leaves everybody blind"—because it is so relevant to the history of violence in Northern Ireland, not just during the Troubles of recent times, but throughout the centuries. Another quote from him which I have also used on numerous occasions is: "If you use the methods of your oppressor, you will end up worse than your oppressor."

I read a huge amount of the writings of Martin Luther King in those days. I am certain that it was no accident that the civil rights movement began here in the sixties, directly inspired, I believe, by the American movement. Six months after the death of Martin Luther King, we in Northern Ireland became involved in our own civil rights struggle against discrimination.

— 2 —

Desperate Injustice

History is a nightmare I am trying to awaken from.
James Joyce

The civil rights movement called into question the fundamental validity of the state in Northern Ireland. It also threatened the Unionists, since the border had been drawn specifically to ensure that there were two Protestants to every one Catholic. The Northern Ireland government, therefore, existed on the basis of desperate injustice and to ask for justice was to question the whole philosophy of the state. Once the movement for equality gained momentum, it led to the inevitable collapse of the governmental system in Northern Ireland.

This was a major victory for the civil rights movement and it led to the establishment of direct rule from London. Throughout the previous fifty or sixty years, Northern Ireland was ruled by one party, without any interference from the London government. Despite the fact that British taxes were paying to maintain the situation and the claim that Northern Ireland was an integral part of the United Kingdom, members of the British parliament were not allowed to ask questions in the House of Commons about Northern Ireland. In fact, in the sixties, a group of Labour MPs—Paul Rose, Stan Orme and Kevin McNamara—campaigned for the democratisation of Ulster, and tried to raise the question in parliament. Astonishingly, they weren't allowed to!

Once the civil rights marches appeared on television worldwide, massive international pressure was brought to bear on the British government. They, in turn, put pressure on the Northern Ireland government to do something about the situation. The Derry Citizens' Action Committee organised civil rights demonstrations on the streets of the city. Within weeks of our starting a major civil rights movement the local city corporation (the city council) was brought down by the government and replaced with an independent commission.

The civil rights movement's strategy of non-violence was greatly influenced by Martin Luther King's philosophy. Don't retaliate, let the world see who the real aggressor is—that was our fundamental message to our fellow marchers when we were attacked by baton-wielding police.

When the British army entered the Bogside in strength after internment was introduced, the residents flocked out onto the streets. It was obvious that there was going to be violence and I foresaw the possibility of many deaths. So I asked the people to sit down. This was always my response to potential trouble on the streets, a simple strategy which generally calmed the atmosphere. Then I addressed the crowd and said, "Your objective is for the army to leave our street. Now, if I negotiate with them and get these troops to withdraw, will you go home?" They agreed.

I approached the commander and said, "If your troops pull out, these local people will go home and there will be no trouble." The commander agreed, but, as they were pulling out from one side, another regiment entered from the other side, and the people thought that I had been tricked. So, again, I told them to sit down, and I spoke to the commander of the second unit and said, "I have arranged with the other commander to have order in our streets. If you guys disappear, the people will go home, but if you stay, there's going to be serious trouble." He said, "I'm in charge here, not you." "Look," I replied, "Don't be talking nonsense, we're talking about order in our streets." He just repeated, "I'm in charge, and you're not."

Having recognised me, it was obvious that he was challenging my authority. If I had given in, I would have lost my authority with the people, so I sat down with them, in front of the soldiers, who then hosed us down with purple dye and brought up a tank. I got up and walked towards them with my hands up, and they repeatedly knocked me down with the jet from the hose. Finally, some soldiers grabbed me and put me up against a wall, where they photographed me, and then they arrested me, charging me with obstructing Her Majesty's forces.

It was soon obvious to them that they had made a terrible mistake, so I was only fined twenty pounds, which I refused to pay. I took the case right up to the House of Lords, expertly advised by my friend and great Belfast lawyer, Charlie Hill. This was a historic constitutional case, known as "Regina versus Hume and Others". My argument in court was that I was arrested under the Northern Ireland Special Powers Act by the British army, but that the British army could only legally operate under acts of their own parliament, and not of the Northern Ireland parliament, which was subsidiary. When I won the case, it made the British army's presence in Northern Ireland illegal. The British government then had to sit up all night retrospectively passing a bill to legalise the presence of their own army in Northern Ireland!

The British Lord Chancellor acknowledged in the House of Lords that there were important implications for Britain from the outcome of the case, as their troops were in the command of the subsidiary government, rather than under direct command. They held secret talks with the Northern Ireland government, insisting that they surrender the power of security to the British government. When the Northern Ireland government refused, the British government suspended Stormont, in March 1972, and imposed direct rule of Northern Ireland from London.

During my involvement with the civil rights movement, I realised that there was no major political party representing those who were not Unionists in Northern Ireland. There was a Nationalist Party, whose genesis had been in reaction to the partition of Ireland in 1920, a response which was totally necessary and understandable at that time. However, by this time the border had been in existence for almost fifty years and our generation realised that the problem was now more complex. While we were concerned about the division among our people, we were also concerned about unemployment and housing and discrimination. With this in mind, we felt that we should have an organised political force to represent us—a party with membership.

I fought my first election for the Northern Ireland parliament in 1969, against the leader of the Nationalist Party, Eddie McAteer, an honourable and highly respected man, who had been a natural leader of his generation. However, I felt that our generation was faced with a whole new situation and I sought a mandate in that election to found a party based on social democratic principles. The fact that I—a young Independent—defeated the leader of the Nationalist Party in that election reflected the massive surge of new political interest among the voters and the arrival of a new generation, the first generation who were the products of public education.

Two other Independent candidates, Paddy O'Hanlon and Ivan Cooper, were also elected, and we immediately began the process of forming a new party. Our success in the election showed the enormous change in mood that had taken place in our community and we believed that there was greater unity among the people than ever before, so we sought to unite as many of the existing small parties as possible within the one new organisation. We contacted Austin Currie, an elected Nationalist, Gerry Fitt of Republican Labour, Paddy Devlin of Northern Ireland Labour, and many other elected representatives who shared a lot of common ground—and so the dialogue began.

Our aim was to form a left-of-centre party that would concentrate on the social and economic needs of the people as well as the deeper political problem. In 1970, after almost a year of talks, the Social Democratic Labour Party (SDLP) was founded, as an organised party with membership right across Northern Ireland. Gerry Fitt was the new party's first leader and I was deputy leader.

From the very beginning the SDLP was happy to include Protestants. In fact, of the three of us who fought the first election as Independents, two were Catholics and one, Ivan Cooper, was Protestant. To this day, senior members of the SDLP are Protestant, as the important issue for our party is human rights, not religion, and our objective is a continuous respect for the rights and traditions of Catholics and Protestants alike. We are both non-sectarian and anti-sectarian.

The first few years of the party's existence were years of accelerating violence, leading up to Bloody Sunday on 30 January 1972. Following the success of the civil rights movement, the Official IRA, as it was known, had announced a very welcome total cessation of violence. Shortly afterwards, a Unionist mob stormed down the Falls Road in Belfast and burnt Bombay Street nearly to the ground, killing nine young Catholics. The following day, written on a wall in Catholic West Belfast, were the words "IRA, I Ran Away". This incident triggered the foundation of what became known as the Provisional IRA, and the re-emergence of Sinn Féin as a political force for Republicans.

Sinn Féin voters traditionally came from Republican families, which had always been associated with the IRA from early in this century. The difference between Republican and Nationalist was that Nationalists worked constitutionally through conventional politics and Republicans believed in physical force and giving their lives for Ireland.

This tradition of Irish Republican nationalism existed from the 1916 period onwards—Pádraig Pearse was part of the emotionalism of Republican mythology—patriotism was about dying for Ireland. However, as I have repeatedly reiterated since 1970, there's a very fine line between dying for Ireland and killing for Ireland.

Most political parties have used flags to whip up emotions. This was never more true than in Northern Ireland. The SDLP, however, has never used flags in this way. We have always been totally opposed to violence, believing that, if the people of Ireland are already divided, further violence will only deepen the divisions and the bitterness, thereby exacerbating the problem. Our task is to work for equality of treatment for all our citizens.

The SDLP, founded in the wake of the civil rights movement, has always concentrated on the issues of inequality, housing and unemployment. Once direct rule from London commenced, the British government was forced to introduce fair play in public employment and in housing. The SDLP leadership proposed to Jim Callaghan, the then British Home Secretary, that, to eliminate discrimination, housing should be taken out of the hands of local authorities and replaced by a central independent housing body. He agreed, and the Northern Ireland Housing Executive was born in February 1971. This body has transformed public housing in Northern Ireland, a significant development brought about by the civil rights movement and the SDLP.

The SDLP has achieved many social reforms. Through our efforts, the voting system has now been changed to proportional representation. Prior to this the system did not allow one-person-one-vote. Limited companies had six votes each and, at one stage, the Unionist mayor of Derry owned seven companies, giving him forty-two votes plus his own! Sadly, the one area where we have been unable to make much progress is in unemployment, mainly because of the violence.

It was a generational change which brought about my election and the formation of the SDLP. Ours was the first generation to benefit from the provision of public education for all and university education, too, producing professional people—lawyers, doctors, teachers—from all walks of life, including the poorest of backgrounds. When the history of Ireland in the twentieth century is written, a major element will be the emergence of a new educated generation from a section of the community that never before had such education. This event cannot be over-emphasised.

Education has brought more active thinking into the whole political arena as well, tackling not only the constitutional question, but also questions of injustice, civil rights, employment and housing—what politics is really about. One of the fundamental arguments which we first put forward, which was a challenge to traditional Nationalist thinking, was that it was people who have rights and not territory. It was not the land of Ireland that was divided, it was the people of Ireland. The line on the map was geographical, but the real border was in the minds and hearts of the people, and that could not be resolved in a week or two. A resolution could only be achieved by consensus, and not by any form of coercion. A healing and evolutionary process is the only way to break down the barriers of history, and our challenge is to create the institutions within which that process will take place.

Part Two

Politics

— 3 —

A Question of Civil Rights

One man can make a difference, but every man should try.
John F. Kennedy

Americans are heirs and beneficiaries of great traditions and principles of constitutional government. These stand out as of particular value and, indeed, as a standard of emulation and application in our own affairs in Ireland today. Through a process of development that was never easy or free of problems, Americans have gone very far in giving real, practical effect to equality before the law for every citizen and to equality of opportunity for all. America is a country where there is a wider measure of national and political consensus, fashioned from rich and broad diversity.

In America, there has always been respect for this idea of unity in diversity and, whatever the controversies may be about the value and application today of the old melting-pot concept, there is increasing acceptance of the idea of cultural pluralism. Not without difficulty or devoid of controversy, Americans have achieved religious tolerance and separation of church and state. Written on the smallest coin is the message of greatest value, the cement of American society—*e pluribus unum*—from many, one. The tragedy of divided people everywhere, as in Ireland, is that they have pushed difference to the point of division and have not yet learned the lesson that the essence of unity in every democratic society in the world is to accept and respect diversity.

Those who come from an Irish-American background come from a community which brought to the building of America qualities encompassed in the poet W. B. Yeats' description "the indomitable Irishry" and left a record of achievement in which they may take justifiable pride. They brought a thirst for justice and an appreciation of the power of organisation, reflected in the development of the labour movement and of popular, democratic politics. They were not all angels but, in the main, they rejected the fatalistic claim that power corrupts, accepting instead the dictum of their fellow countryman George Bernard Shaw, "Fools corrupt power". They understood and applied the use of power, of politics, for good as, just over thirty years ago, John F. Kennedy and Robert Kennedy embraced the vision of Martin Luther King to develop and apply the powers of the federal government in the interests of justice and equality for African-Americans.

Irish-Americans have also understood and put to good use the power of education—its power for the material and social advancement of the individual and of his or her community. They did not seek to improve their position in American society through violence or through any attempt to obtain or exercise a dominant position. Instead they harnessed the non-violent power of education, first saving from their meagre incomes as labourers or servants the money that was necessary to educate their sons and daughters, and later applying the resources of any improved position to endow institutions of education and to support investment, economic and social development and cultural activity in Ireland itself. All this progress without throwing a stone.

The progress of the Irish in America from a background of starving immigrants and deep deprivation to positions of power and influence in all walks of American life is one of the greatest success stories of non-violence in the Western world. In Northern Ireland, the people of Irish Nationalist tradition whom I represent have followed the same path. We also shared that thirst and respect for education and when, after World War II, the policies of the British Labour government greatly widened access to education, we seized the opportunities thus afforded.

A new and highly educated generation emerged from the Nationalist minority, as it also emerged among the Irish in America and more lately among African-Americans. They were not prepared to accept intolerance and disadvantage as their legacy or as a future for their children. That new generation embarked on a struggle to achieve equal rights in the North of Ireland, including the right to have their political and cultural tradition reflected and expressed in the structures by which they were governed. The methods chosen by the great majority of them were those of non-violent protest and of democratic politics which have served so well for both the Irish- and African-Americans.

The story of Northern Ireland is a story of conflict, not of religious conflict—even though the two communities who live there draw much of their character and their coherence from their religious traditions. It is rather a conflict between the aspirations of ordinary men and women—600,000 Nationalists, 900,000 Unionists—who have been trapped by a tragic error of history which saw their hopes and fears as mutually exclusive and irreconcilable within an Irish state, but which obliged them nonetheless to live and compete side-by-side in one small corner of Ireland. These two communities in Northern Ireland, Catholic and Protestant, Nationalist and Unionist, have both behaved like threatened minorities and only by removing the fears which they both feel can a just and durable solution be found.

Northern Ireland was born out of the insecurity of the Protestant–Unionist minority in Ireland itself. Fearful of becoming a minority in the Irish state then emerging seventy years ago, distrustful of the intentions of their fellow Irish people, and zealous to protect the advantages they believed they had under British rule, the leadership of the Unionist community sought and achieved, through threat of force, the acquiesence of Britain in the creation of a new political, territorial and artificial entity in Ireland wherein they hoped they could shape their own destiny as part of the United Kingdom. But the new self-governing political entity thereby established, called Northern Ireland, was neither secure nor homogeneous. Caught within its boundaries was a substantial Catholic and Nationalist minority which felt itself Irish, and which did not cease to be Irish simply because legislation elsewhere had drawn a line on a map and declared that henceforth they were British. Thus Northern Ireland served only to extend and aggravate this conflict by compressing the clash of majority and minority within an even more narrow and more rigid territorial, economic and social confine. As Yeats saw it:

> Great hatred, little room,
> Maimed us at the start.

For over fifty years the Unionist majority sought to entrench their position through political gerrymandering and discrimination. Though inexcusable, it was inevitable that they should have acted in this fashion—as other majorities have at times acted—since their inheritance was not a land of promise but a polity of insecurity. It was inevitable also that each attempt they made, at the expense of their neighbours, to strengthen their role and protect their privileges should serve only to disrupt the structures of society as a whole and to create new tensions and new insecurities. This was the case also in the Deep South of the United States not too many years ago where an insensitive and insecure white majority held sway. I have already referred to the parallel emergence in Northern Ireland and in the American south of a new articulate generation whose expectations were raised through education and who were impatient and angry at the injustices they suffered.

The American civil rights movement in the 1960s gave birth to ours. Their successes were for us a cause of hope. The songs of their movement were also ours. We also believe that "we shall overcome"; that rallying song is sung every year at my party conference. Most importantly, the philosophy of non-violence which sustained their struggle was also part of ours. Our own history and our own circumstances gave a special power to the counsel of Martin Luther King that violence as a way of achieving justice is both impractical and immoral. As he put it:

> It is impractical because it is a descending spiral ending in destruction for all. The old law of an eye for an eye leaves everybody blind. It is immoral because it seeks to humiliate the opponent rather than win understanding; it seeks to annihilate rather than convert. Violence is immoral because it thrives on hatred rather than love. It destroys community and makes brotherhood impossible. It leaves society in monologue rather than dialogue. Violence ends by defeating itself. It creates bitterness in the survivors and brutality in the destroyers.

Can anyone looking at divided societies in the world today doubt the wisdom of these words of Martin Luther King?

The world in the 1960s responded with sympathy to our non-violent movement for civil rights as it did to America's. But whereas in the United States the structures of democracy were resilient enough to encompass the challenge of civil rights, in the unstable political environment of Northern Ireland, our struggle was perceived as a threat to the very survival of the society itself and as such was resisted by the institutions of the state. In the ensuing clash, the Unionist majority, through the imposition of direct rule from London, lost their local parliament which they had come to regard as the symbol of their independence and as the guarantor of their heritage. Though many would still wish to regard Northern Ireland as their exclusive homeland, they lack the power and indeed the freedom to shape their destiny as they once hoped. Though they dominate the security institutions of the state still, they have not found security as a people. This insecurity has led them to oppose change, even when that change is constructive.

Nevertheless, through pressure on the British government, including the presence of sympathetic opinion in America and the world at large, we were able to make, through non-violent methods, major progress on a number of fronts, especially on the original demands of our civil rights movement. These included one-person-one-vote, fair allocation of public housing and an end to job discrimination. Before that, gerrymandering was rife in Northern Ireland and local elections and unfair voting systems were used by the Unionist ascendancy to control housing and jobs on a sectarian basis. Housing conditions in many parts of the North were appalling. Today the housing situation throughout Northern Ireland has been transformed due to the creation of the Northern Ireland Housing Executive. This proposal took public housing allocation out of the hands of local Unionist politicians. This has meant a major transformation in the living conditions of people throughout Northern Ireland.

The electoral and local government systems have been drastically altered with the introduction of proportional representation, ending gerrymandering at the local level and reducing the power of political bigots. A public regulatory agency, the Fair Employment Commission, for which we fought successfully but for which we want more teeth, is and has been a valuable watchdog in exposing, and making more difficult, discrimination by public bodies and the private sector.

We made very worthwhile advances which improved the lives of ordinary men and women. However, we encountered a blockage from the Unionist parties to our legitimate calls and efforts to secure for Nationalist people the right to effective political, symbolic and administrative expression of their identity, including a fair share in the exercise of political power in the executive, as well as the legislative branch of government. The reforms we secured were not, regrettably, generously and openly offered by the majority party but had to be imposed on them by the British government and parliament.

Against the background of the resulting clashes and in impatience at the results achieved by peaceful, political methods, the philosophy of non-violence was rejected by a minority in my own community. They followed the old law of an eye for an eye, and in the end were inevitably brutalised by the process in which they were engaged. In their savage anger and barbarous deeds, they came to reflect in themselves all of the hatred and sectarianism they had sought to overthrow. In their pursuit of violence, they demeaned the cause we hold dear and lost us many good allies around the world. Sustained by their violence this group seemed beset by the illusion that they could, one day, impose their will on Ireland as a whole.

This violence, together with the Unionist intransigence which gave it birth and the too long continued inadequacies of British policies in tackling the underlying political problem, has left us a bitter harvest. The human losses and economic costs have been enormous. The most tragic loss is the deaths of over 3,000 men, women and children. These deaths, in an area with a population of one and a half million, are equivalent in proportionate terms to the killing of approximately 350,000 in the United States. In addition, almost 25,000 people have been injured or maimed. Thousands are suffering from psychological stress because of the fear and tension generated by murder, bombing, intimidation and the impact of security countermeasures. In Northern Ireland, we now have the highest number of prisoners per head of population in Western Europe—in an area where, thirty years ago, serious crime was practically unknown.

The lives of tens of thousands have been deeply affected. The effect on society has been shattering. There is hardly a family that has not been touched to some degree by death, injury or intimidation.

I would quote Martin Luther King again:

> When an individual is no longer a true participant, when he no longer feels a sense of responsibility to his society, the content of democracy is emptied...when the social system does not build security but induces peril, inexorably the individual is impelled to pull away from a soulless society. This produces alienation—perhaps the most pervasive and insidious development in contemporary society.

Although a consequence of the injustice of others, alienation is a desperate development within minorities because it weakens their coherence, erodes their faith in progress and gives violence the opportunity to take root. As it was expressed by W. B. Yeats, and none have said it better, "Too long a sacrifice can make a stone of the heart."

When a society produces alienation in the individual, when it cannot provide for the equality and the differences of its citizens, "when the social system does not build security but induces peril", that society must be reshaped and transformed through new institutions which accommodate diversity and promote the best basis for reconciliation.

This is the only way forward in Northern Ireland. Let me demonstrate this by considering briefly the alternatives offered. There is the traditional Unionist approach, of seeking the exclusive exercise of political power in Northern Ireland for themselves, of ignoring the existence of a community, comprising forty per cent of the area's population, who have a different identity and a different aspiration.

They hark back to the past and speak of the future only with fear and foreboding, a paranoia encapsulated by a poet in the lines now taken up in graffiti on the walls of the area's largest city:

> To hell with the future and long live the past,
> May God in his mercy be kind to Belfast.

One can join in saying "Amen" to the last line but the conflict reflects a sad condition, a siege mentality, rooted in insecurity, in prejudice, in fear of domination by a Catholic majority in Ireland, so-called "Rome Rule", a bitter play on "Home Rule" which was a policy of self-autonomy rejected by Unionists in 1912. Even if, in the light of history and of the violent campaign of the IRA, some of these fears are understandable, they are groundless. There can be no solution to our problem which seeks to destroy or to crush the Protestant heritage in Ireland. It would be unthinkable. Accommodation of difference is the only basis for peace and stability in our divided society. I have always avowed that simple truth.

Then there is the other alternative, that of the Provisional IRA and Sinn Féin. For twenty-five years we in the SDLP have opposed the IRA. We have pointed out in critical statements of their actions that the IRA has bombed factories while Sinn Féin shouts about unemployment; that the IRA shot a teacher in a classroom, killed schoolbus drivers, killed people on campuses, and then Sinn Féin lectures us about education; that the IRA maimed and injured, and carried out attacks in hospital precincts while Sinn Féin talks about protecting the Health Service. The real strategy and objectives were clear. In our view, the IRA created as much discontent and deprivation as possible, including unemployment. Then Sinn Féin was trying to feed off the people's discontent.

My party, the SDLP, born out of the civil rights movement, long ago rejected these two purported alternatives which in fact offer no hope for the future. Like Martin

Luther King, we had a dream; like Theobald Wolfe Tone, the father of Irish republicanism, our vision has been "to substitute for the denomination of Catholic, Protestant and Dissenter the common name of Irishman". Our chosen strategy encompassed reform, reconciliation, and reunification along a path of steady progress, continually narrowing the gap between the reality and the dream, using the political means of dialogue, persuasion, negotiation, accommodation, compromise. Violence can never heal the deep wounds that divide a people. Only a healing process can in time end the division in Ireland. And it will take time.

Our analysis is that the first necessary step in that healing process is the creation of total equality of treatment of all the citizens of Northern Ireland, Nationalists and Unionists alike, from basic civil rights to full expression of their identity. I have outlined the worthwhile—but still far from adequate—reforms and changes achieved in earlier stages of this reform process. But even after these, Nationalists in Northern Ireland remained within a state with which they could not identify. Its institutions, security system, cultural assumptions and official symbolism were alien to them and appeared in many ways designed to make them strangers in their own land, in a situation where they were denied any constructive means of expressing their Irish identity and aspirations, their cultural and political identification with the rest of Ireland. Thus, the process of bringing about practical recognition and respect for equality between the two identities and communities remains to be completed. To achieve this was the first objective we set for ourselves.

On the basis of that equality, because reconciliation can only be based on equality, comes the process of reconciliation, the second element in my party's long-term programme, the breaking down of barriers between the different sections of our people. No one can underestimate the difficulty of that task. It will take time, but it is a task that involves everyone and that will lead, coming to the third major element, to the only Irish unity that really matters, the only unity that all pre-partition leaders spoke of, a unity that respects diversity and legitimises differences. That is a process and objective that no one need fear because everyone must be part of the building process. Those who claim that their role and objective in politics are to preserve, protect and develop the Protestant tradition in Ireland have surely much more interest in a process such as this than standing forever apart, paranoid about the future precisely because they have refused to grasp the nettle of settling their relationships with the people with whom they share the island of Ireland.

Central to the strategy of the SDLP over the years has been that the problem can best be resolved if the framework of the solution is the framework of the problem. We argued for years that the British and Irish governments should work together in an organised fashion to tackle the problem and, in a policy document in 1981, we suggested the creation of a British–Irish council of ministers, serviced by a joint secretariat and backed up by a British–Irish parliamentary tier. That eventually emerged in the Anglo-Irish Agreement of 1985.

The process of reform and reconciliation can best be tackled through a framework corresponding to the framework of the problem and thus, through the British–Irish framework, through an approach that deals with the three major dimensions of the problem—relations between the two communities in Northern Ireland, relations between both parties, the Nationalist and Unionist traditions in Ireland as a whole, and relations between Ireland and Britain. The Unionists have to be brought to see that they cannot defy the will of the British parliament to which they profess loyalty, as they did successfully in 1912 when they prevented Home Rule from being established, and after the Sunningdale Agreement in 1974 when they brought an end to the power-sharing local government which had been introduced. They have to be brought to realise that they cannot have matters all their own way. In this way they could be liberated from the prison into which they have locked themselves and, one hopes, led to embrace true politics which they have been able to eschew up to now—largely like the whites in the southern United States. The whites would never have been liberated without the intervention of the federal government. They would never have liberated themselves.

When they are ready to do so, I and my party stand ready to meet Unionists and engage in discussions on how we share our future together. We must begin the process of breaking down the barriers between us, barriers of prejudice and distrust which are at the heart of the conflict that has disfigured Ireland for centuries. We have a choice. We can live together or live apart. We have lived apart for too long and we have seen the bitter consequences. Or we can live together with all the painful readjustments that this will require. It is the only road to peace and stability, for whatever happens we will be sharing the same piece of earth for a long, long time.

My party wishes to demonstrate the potential of democratic politics and of the philosophy of non-violence to make progress toward the resolution of what is perhaps one of the more intractable political problems in the world today. I believe that these same principles are applicable in the field of international relations. When we are dealing with human conflict whether in a divided community, a divided country or a divided globe, it is the building of mutual trust and not mutual fear that will solve the problem of conflict—not just in Ireland, but around the world—because we know that human beings are no different wherever they live.

Part Three

Reconciliation

— 4 —

British Policy in Northern Ireland

No man has the right to fix the boundary of the march of a nation.

Charles Stewart Parnell

As a practising politician throughout the recent twenty-five-year cycle of conflict in Northern Ireland, I have taken a particular interest while travelling abroad in following the world media coverage of the problem. For the most part, this has been a chronicle of atrocities reported spasmodically from London. It has struck me that, for the outside observer, it must have been difficult during these years to avoid the impression that Northern Ireland was hopelessly sunk in incoherence and its people the victims of a particularly opaque political pathology. There have, it is true, been a few brief interludes when some measure of clarity seemed to take hold, only to be swept away in the inevitable swirling clouds of violence, intransigence and misery—in other words, the normal political climate.

The people of Northern Ireland, however divided, share a keen awareness of the bewilderment of outsiders. Winston Churchill's World War II Dunkirk exhortation, "The situation is serious but not desperate," is said to have evoked the somewhat bleary comment from an Irish listener, "Over here the situation is always desperate but never serious." The cynicism and dismissiveness of the Irish style often conceal, as the readers of Swift and Joyce know well, a quite serious desperation. Nevertheless, in its superficial manifestation, the hopeless wit of the people proved congenial to those who are currently responsible for the affairs of Northern Ireland, and who, of all "outside" observers, often seem the most puzzled and wearied by its problem, i.e., the British political establishment. This is nothing new. It was, in fact, Churchill, speaking in the House of Commons in 1922, who most eloquently caught this feeling of his colleagues, then and since:

> Then came the Great War. Every institution, almost, in the world was strained. Great empires have been overturned. The whole map of Europe has been changed...The mode of thought of men, the whole outlook on affairs, the grouping of parties, all have encountered violent and tremendous changes in the deluge of the world, but as the deluge subsides and the waters fall, we see the dreary steeples of Fermanagh and Tyrone emerging once again. The integrity of their quarrel is one of the few institutions that have been unaltered in the cataclysm which has swept the world.

Other cataclysms have since supervened, and are themselves now forgotten, but "their quarrel" endures, for the past generation in a more grisly form than ever. The skilled and the professionally trained emigrate while the economy stagnates, and the semi-skilled and unskilled swell the unemployment lines, as they have swollen the ranks of the paramilitary organisations.

However, events unleashed a chilling shower, drenching Irish and British alike, from which the flippant, patronising and slightly amused attitudes of the past afforded no refuge whatever.

One of the difficulties about Northern Ireland which existed until recently was that the problem seemed to matter little, if at all. It mattered very little to the British and seemed incapable of sustaining the attention of any but the most committed fanatics. Governments and serious observers, if they looked at it, had a feeling of impatience with its complexities, its anthill of competing eccentricities. There was a feeling that it ought to be like the pieces of a jigsaw, needing only to be placed in a certain arrangement for tranquillity to ensue. Unfortunately, the pieces did not seem to fit, and the puzzle quickly lost its interest.

It is my strong conviction, as well as that of the Social Democratic and Labour Party, that the politics of Northern Ireland are not hopelessly irrational. They do have a meaning and a structure. The protagonists do act in the light of their interests as they perceive them, though their perceptions are sometimes mistaken. Events are, in fact, predictable—often, it must be admitted, depressingly so.

My conviction that there exist structure and meaning, and therefore hope, is not based simply on Henry Kissinger's moral injunction to statespeople that they must at all costs believe in the possibility of solutions to the most intractable impasses. I also believe that the perennial British view of the problem as "their quarrel" and not "ours" is fundamentally wrong: Britain is, in fact, included in the quarrel as a central protagonist, and must be centrally involved in the solution. It is for the acceptance of this principle that I and my party have worked for years.

The problem, as I know from years of talking to foreign visitors, is at first sight a mass of contradictions. Some of the contradictions are real. London, for its part, exercises a reluctant sovereignty in Northern Ireland, while Dublin maintains a somewhat reluctant claim to that sovereignty. The "Loyalists" are those proponents of the union with Britain who, while they are avowedly the most patriotic of all Her Majesty's subjects, put up the most stubborn resistance to her government's designs. The Provisional wing of the Irish Republican Army believed Irish unity would be secured by waging war against a British establishment which clearly has no fundamental opposition to unity, while they ignored those who most adamantly resist the imposition of unity, the 900,000 Protestant majority. The contradictions further underline the necessity, reinforced by horrific events, that all major parties to this crisis should rigorously re-examine their own roles, responsibilities and room for manoeuvre.

The basis of British policy is concealed under layers of good intentions, ingenious initiatives, commissions of enquiry, attempted reforms, financial aid and a good deal of genial bewilderment. I do not use the word "concealed" maliciously. Many sincere and concerned British politicians and observers have the impression that they have tried everything possible to get the Irish to agree: that is a measure of the extent to which the basic assumption of their policy has become imperceptible to the British themselves.

The only ground of their policy is the reiterated guarantee that Northern Ireland shall remain a part of the United Kingdom as long as a majority of the electorate of Northern Ireland so desire. That would seem, at first reading, to be an eminently democratic and responsible undertaking. The fact is, however, that it has not worked. It has not produced peace or stable government in Northern Ireland. Moreover, it has provided the basis for nearly seventy-five years of injustice, discrimination and repressive law, a situation in which the minority community (the Catholics) have been the persistent losers and victims.

Northern Ireland is a divided community, divided not by theological differences but by conflicting aspirations. The Unionist majority historically favour maintenance of the union with Britain, while the Nationalist minority by and large favour a united Ireland. In 1921, when the overwhelmingly Catholic Nationalist Free State was established in the south, the area of Northern Ireland was excluded from the arrangement, because of British hesitancy (which proved to be an enduring feature of British policy) in the face of militant Protestant Unionist resistance.

The British guarantee, as it is called, has proved to be a guarantee of permanent exclusive power to one side, the Unionists, and a guarantee of permanent exclusion from power to the other, the Catholic minority. Its existence undermines any hope of political negotiation between the two sides in Northern Ireland. It guarantees the integrity of "their" quarrel. While this guarantee exists, there is no incentive for Unionists to enter into genuine dialogue with those with whom they share the island of Ireland. The suffering and frustration of the people of Northern Ireland overwhelmingly attest to the fact that the guarantee was, to put it very bluntly, a tragic mistake. The price has been paid too long, and in too many lives.

Northern Ireland is an unnatural enclave—the border was drawn to give two Protestants to every Catholic. It has reenforced the laager mentality of the Unionist people, whose answer is to hold all power in their own hands—to exclude everyone else. This mentality has caused widespread discrimination. Majority rule in that situation is not democracy, because it is an unnatural majority. We have argued strongly that we need a new system of government that has the allegiance of both sections of the community and we were the first party to come forward with the whole notion of power-sharing.

Many attempts at reform, in which so much British as well as Irish energy was invested, failed. One initiative that almost succeeded was the Sunningdale Agreement of 1973 between the British and Irish governments and the principal parties in Northern Ireland. This established a power-sharing government containing representatives of both sections of the community in Northern Ireland and accepted the principle of a Council of Ireland. The Council would provide a forum for north–south co-operation as well as a means of expression for the Irish Nationalist aspiration, while Northern Ireland would continue to be a part of the United Kingdom.

The British government of Ted Heath made a major effort at getting consensus. The Sunningdale Agreement for the first time set up a mixed government in Northern Ireland. There was to be a council of ministers, an equal number from north and south, who would work together on areas of common interest, but only by agreement. That government went into operation in 1974 but lasted only five months. I was Minister of Commerce, which made me responsible for industrial development during that period. The government was, in my opinion, very successful because trust was building among the people sitting in that government in a way that it had never done before.

The establishment of power-sharing was a tribute to the political courage and imagination of the then Conservative government in Britain. Unfortunately, the Labour administration which succeeded it early in 1974 showed no similar courage, and in May of that year, in what was one of the most squalid examples of government irresponsibility, it surrendered its policy in the face of a political strike organised by a paramilitary minority on the Unionist side. The Unionist paramilitaries called the Ulster Workers' Council strike which was supported by the Unionist Party, and Dr. Ian Paisley, who had refused to support the section of the Unionist Party involved in the new government.

The British government of the day backed down to the strike instead of standing firm as they should have done. In my opinion, it would not have meant using any force. The vast majority did not go on strike, but the one area where the strike worked was in the electricity services. We did not think the strike could last very long under the circumstances and the government should have been able to provide the essential services.

Unfortunately, this political cowardice of the government was a disaster because extreme unionism or loyalism was encouraged in its belief that it could henceforth resist and jettison any British policy for Northern Ireland which involved conceding power to the minority. By so vindicating the Unionist approach of exclusivity, the British served to underwrite the maintenance of sectarian solidarity and negativism as the basic method of Unionist politics. They also served to convince sections of the Nationalist community that violence was the best approach to take against the British; political approaches would only be frustrated by what we call the "Orange Card".

That is the nub of political deadlock in Northern Ireland. Only when the "Orange Card" of threat, violence and sectarianism is denied political currency can that deadlock really be broken. This requires the creation of an alternative approach by Britain and a more politic, positive and realistic approach by Nationalist Ireland.

When Sunningdale collapsed, once again there was no system of government in Northern Ireland. It was a political vacuum leading to obvious instability. There was violence on both sides, but throughout, we in the SDLP continued to try to seek a solution, based on agreement between our divided people and based on the approach of getting institutions of government together. In order to bring that about a convention was established to which all parties were elected. The purpose of that convention was to reach agreement, but again it failed. There was a further attempt in 1979 by the new Secretary of State, Sir Humphrey Atkins, to bring the parties around the table to try to reach agreement, and once again, total failure.

We concluded that the reason we were continually failing to reach agreement was that we were not discussing the real problem. All that was happening was that parties in Northern Ireland were meeting to discuss affairs in Northern Ireland. But the real problem wasn't just relations within Northern Ireland, it was a British–Irish problem. It was the failure of Britain and Ireland to resolve their differences in the 1920s and they pushed the failure into a corner called Northern Ireland. We argued that the time had come for both governments to work together to solve the problem.

Until then relations between British and Irish governments were a matter of what we call "megaphone diplomacy". We reckoned that if we were going to solve this problem peacefully, and if the problem involved all relationships within Northern Ireland and the Republic of Ireland, and between Britain and Ireland, the proper approach was to get all energies harnessed to resolving it. That meant the British and Irish governments working together and that became central to our policy and our approach. We put our opinion very strongly to the Dublin government, that we should be approaching the British government with a view to getting a joint approach to resolving this problem.

The first major step on that road was agreeing in 1981 to set up the Anglo-Irish Intergovernmental Council. These efforts suffered a severe setback almost immediately, as a result of the trauma arising from the campaign and deaths of the hunger-strikers imprisoned in Northern Ireland. As a consequence, we faced a bleak situation and prospect, with alienation greatly accentuated and more widespread among all sections of the Nationalist community and with the political situation apparently in a state of deadlock and paralysis.

During the 1980s, the British government had another election for a Northern Assembly. We decided we would not take part in the new assembly because it was not dealing with the overall problem, and all the relationships would just be the same as all the previous assemblies. Instead, my party took a fresh initiative at that stage, designed to break the log-jam and to carry our analysis into the realm of practical politics. We put forward a proposal which came to fruition as the New Ireland Forum, a deliberative body of elected representatives from the four major constitutional Nationalist parties in Ireland, both north and south, representing over ninety per cent of the Nationalist population of Ireland. Set up by Irish Taoiseach Garret FitzGerald, the purpose of the Forum was to hold consultations on the manner in which lasting peace and stability could be achieved in a new Ireland through the democratic process and to report on possible new structures and a process through which this objective might be achieved. In other words, we sought to outline a modern up-to-date and formal statement or blueprint, setting out the principles and structures on the basis of which the constitutional Nationalist dream of a new Ireland could be achieved. Through the New Ireland Forum we laid the groundwork for the Irish Nationalist approach following the beginnings of a new framework between Britain and Ireland. It was the first time since 1920 that Nationalist Ireland had sat down to examine intensively its attitudes to a resolution of the problem.

After a process of scientific study, public hearings and political debate and compromise, that body produced, in May 1984, an agreed Report which attracted widespread acclaim and support, including that of the then President Reagan and the United States Congress, in a concurring resolution of both Houses, the first on Irish affairs since the 1920s. Against the background of a fresh and generous assessment of the realities of the situation, this Report proposed ten key and necessary elements of a framework within which a new Ireland could emerge. These proposals were firmly rooted in the concept of unity in diversity. Indeed, the kernel of the Report was set out in one of its paragraphs, as follows:

> The solution to both the historic problem and the current crisis of Northern Ireland and the continuing problem of relations between Ireland and Britain necessarily requires new structures that will accommodate together two sets of legitimate rights: the right of Nationalists to effective political, symbolic and administrative expression of their identity; and the right of Unionists to effective political, symbolic and administrative expression of their identity, their ethos and their way of life.

The Report of the New Ireland Forum was adopted as policy by the Irish government and taken as the basis for a process of negotiation with the British government. It set out principles and realities that should govern any solution and it became a basis for a real dialogue between the two governments. In addition to putting forward the principles and realities, it put forward three different suggested solutions: a unitary state for the whole of Ireland, a federal state, or a joint sovereignty. There was also a fourth suggestion that we would be prepared to look at any other proposals that might meet those principles and realities. British Prime Minister Margaret Thatcher responded to the Forum's first three suggestions with an emphatic "out, out, out". But it was the fourth suggestion which led to the dialogue between Garret FitzGerald and the British government, which culminated in a formal international agreement between the two countries about Northern Ireland. The Anglo-Irish Agreement was signed on 15 November 1985, at Hillsborough in Northern Ireland, by Garret FitzGerald and Margaret Thatcher.

Though no one among us felt it was the final solution, the Agreement was a major achievement of democratic politics, and was a significant step forward on the road to lasting peace and stability. The Agreement tackled the problem of alienation head on and sought to secure, in line with the central requirement identified in the Report of the New Ireland Forum, equal recognition and respect for both the Nationalist and Unionist traditions. Nationalists could now finally raise their heads knowing their position was, and was seen to be, on an equal footing with that of Unionists.

The Agreement provided, in an arrangement reflecting the particular and unique situation in Northern Ireland, for the establishment by the British and Irish governments of an intergovernmental conference concerned with Northern Ireland and with relations between the two parts of Ireland. In the Agreement, the British government accepted that the Irish government would put forward views and proposals on matters relating to Northern Ireland within the field of activity of the conference. The British government, together with the Irish government, agreed that in the interest of promoting peace and stability, determined efforts would be made to resolve any differences through the conference. The range of issues within the conference's field of activity comprised most of the matters in which the public authorities of a state exercise responsibility, including political, security, legal, economic, social and cultural matters. The conference was to be serviced on a continuing basis by a joint secretariat located in Belfast whose role was to prepare and follow up the conference's work.

We strongly welcomed the Anglo-Irish Agreement when it came out, because it was the first time that there was any such agreement between the two governments to commit themselves to working together. We pointed out that the Agreement was not a solution, but the framework within which a solution could be found. We have been working in that framework ever since.

The provisions in the Agreement, going beyond a consultative role but falling short of an executive role for the Irish government, took nothing away from the legitimate rights of Unionists. Northern Ireland continues to be governed, as Unionists still wish, by the British government. The Agreement rather added a dimension which, by giving institutional recognition to the Irish identity of those of the Nationalist tradition, without detriment to the identity of Unionists, enabled Nationalists to participate fully in the affairs of Northern Ireland without prejudice to their aspirations to Irish unity.

The Agreement secured the support of substantial majorities of the population in Britain and in the Republic of Ireland. It was greeted with satisfaction by a majority of Nationalists in Northern Ireland, although there was, among many, a consciousness that much depended on its practical implementation, with firmness and fairness, by both governments. Internationally, there was unprecedented support, including that of President Reagan and both the House and Senate of the United States Congress.

However, there was a strong negative and hostile reaction among Unionists in Northern Ireland. The Unionist political parties embarked on a determined effort to set the Agreement at nought, even, if necessary, by making Northern Ireland ungovernable. One may regard this opposition from a community used to having all power in their own hands as understandable, even as inevitable, but it is certainly not justifiable. The Agreement took nothing away from the rights or concrete interests of Unionists, nor did it diminish in any way their political, cultural or spiritual heritage.

Particular opposition was expressed to the Irish government having a role in regard to the affairs and administration of Northern Ireland. This attitude ignored the identity and aspirations of the Nationalist people who constitute about forty per cent of the area's population. If there was an apprehension that the role of the Dublin government represented the thin end of the wedge pushing towards a united Ireland against the wishes of a majority, the answer was in the second major feature of the Agreement itself. This recognised, in a binding international instrument, that which is a matter of fact, that Irish unity will only come about with the agreement of a majority of the people of Northern Ireland and that the present wish of a majority is for no change in that status.

The two governments also declared that, if in the future a majority of the people of Northern Ireland clearly wish for and formally consent to the establishment of a united Ireland, they will introduce and support in their respective parliaments legislation to give effect to that wish. Thus the Article of the Agreement devoted to the status of Northern Ireland recognised the identity and aspirations of both traditions there. It also made it implicitly clear that Britain has no interest of her own, strategic or otherwise, in remaining in Ireland and that Irish unity is a matter for those Irish people who want it persuading those Irish people who do not. This should make evident to Nationalists that their method should be to address the question of difference in Ireland and the fears of Unionists rather than engage in violence nominally aimed at the British but in reality maiming the Irish people themselves. The Agreement removed any justification whatsoever for the use of violence. You cannot unite people at the point of a gun.

The Agreement gave Nationalists the opportunity to create advances that could never be achieved through slogans, violence or political non-involvement, while challenging Unionists to create new relationships which would not only protect but enhance their heritage by allowing expression of the Protestant identity without the corruption of exclusivism. The Agreement clearly placed the responsibility on the British government to address properly those matters of legislative offence, administrative insensitivity and legal injustice which infringed the rights of citizens and communities in Northern Ireland. The two sovereign governments undertook to resolve such problems and create ongoing progress in British–Irish relations as a backdrop to improving the political climate within Northern Ireland itself.

Unionist reaction to the Agreement revealed yet another attempt to play the "Orange Card". They came out onto the streets in their thousands to bring it down. By standing firm with the development of new relations between Britain and Ireland and by standing by the commitment to achieving equality in Northern Ireland, the British government served to trump the "Orange Card" and eased the deadlock in Northern Ireland's politics.

If anything jeopardised the Unionist position inside the UK, it was not the Agreement itself but Unionist reaction to the Agreement. The Agreement stated the clear fact that Northern Ireland would remain in the UK as long as a majority of its citizens so wish. That was hardly a threat to the rights of Unionists. It specifically recognised the particular identity and aspirations of the Unionist community. That was hardly "stealing their birthright".

Unionist politicians seemed to object because membership of the UK would no longer be solely on the terms demanded by them. They opposed it because it also gave recognition to the Nationalist identity and the reality of the rightful interest of southern Ireland in the affairs of the North. They suspected it because they recognised that it shifted the unconditional veto from them and perhaps because it offered a process of reconciliation which could lead to a real unity of the Irish people. Sadly they failed, or refused, to see that they had nothing to fear from that process and much to gain. That refusal was not a failure of the Anglo-Irish Agreement; it was an indictment of the past approaches which had created that Unionist mind-set.

Just as it was not stealing anything from Unionists, nor was the Agreement selling anything out for Nationalists. It gave recognition in an international agreement to the Irish identity of people living in Northern Ireland. It committed the two sovereign governments to a process of ensuring equality between the two traditions. It contained an undertaking from the British government to comply fully with any wish for a united Ireland expressed by a majority of citizens there.

Everything that has happened in the past few years stems from the Anglo-Irish Agreement of 1985. The setting up of a permanent secretariat for regular contact established close contacts between the two governments and many issues that could have caused major problems were averted because the governments were talking to each other every day.

It is worth also pointing out that the change in the historic British position is not just a matter for direct clarification by the British government. That government is now committed to it in international agreements with other governments. The European Union commits all its members to an "ever closer union" among the peoples of Europe. That includes an ever closer union between the people of Ireland, north and south, and between Ireland and Britain. Borders are gone all over Europe, including in fact the Irish border. No border means free movement of goods, people and services. The activity that will arise from this will consistently break down the real border in Ireland, which is in the hearts and minds of our people.

The structures established by the Anglo-Irish Agreement reflected those of the European Union. That was no accident. I serve in the European Parliament with representatives of peoples who lived in enduring enmity and in this century alone have killed each other by the million in bitter conflict. If political structures such as those of Europe can be developed to allow people with such a bitter history to work together, exchange concerns and ideas and grow together, addressing their common problems but protecting their essential diversity, then surely the same can happen in the island of Ireland and between Ireland and Britain.

The intergovernmental conference established by the Anglo-Irish Agreement was charged to address and resolve important problems in Northern Ireland and could work to promote co-operation and co-ordination of policies in both parts of Ireland for the benefit of the entire island. Comprised of ministers from both governments it was the equivalent of the European Council of Ministers. Its secretariat was analogous to the European Commission. The Agreement also provided for an inter-parliamentary tier comprising elected representatives of political parties in Britain, Northern Ireland and the Republic of Ireland. Through this feature, broader considerations and criticisms than those of the two governments could enhance the operation and development of the process offered by the Anglo-Irish framework. This parliamentary tier had a role similar to that of the European parliament.

Nobody had anything to fear from such a process. They had much to contribute and much to gain. For the first time the rights and needs of both traditions in Northern Ireland were clearly recognised in a political framework which represented the peoples of both Ireland and Britain. It provided a framework in which we could grow together politically rather than stagnate in sloganising, prejudice, fear and suspicion. If Unionists or Nationalists with their proud traditions really had confidence in themselves and their identities, they would have realised that such a process held no danger for them. If they were afraid then they lacked self-confidence in the values and ideals which they articulated. There could be no progress in subscribing to demands for political arrangements based solely on their political inadequacies. The only possible way forward was for the two sovereign governments to maintain and develop that framework which actually measured up to the full dimensions of the problem and which could give the people of Northern Ireland in particular the room to grow together.

One of the tests of political leadership in this community is to accept the discipline of trying to reach both sides of the community simultaneously. Many have failed this test and many continue to do so. After all, it is easy to appeal to one side to the exclusion of the other: it is not difficult to gratify one side by encouraging its prejudices about the other. It is difficult, sometimes virtually impossible, to bring to each side a sense of the dilemma felt by the other. Yet we know that, until our leaders and our people manage that breakthrough, we will not make progress in Northern Ireland.

We know what must be done, yet history and circumstance seem so often, in both sections of our community, to conspire against us. I believe that we can only understand our situation and grasp our opportunities if the responsibility of Britain is realised and acknowledged. Britain created Northern Ireland, Britain is in charge of Northern Ireland, and it cannot now be regarded as a remote and benign referee whose well-intentioned whistle the participants no longer hear in the din of conflict. Britain is as responsible today for our situation as it was in 1921 and there will be no resolution until it, like us, takes a new view of the interests of all of us.

Northern Ireland today represents unfinished business in the ancient conflict between our two islands. It represents the residual area of failure of the peoples of the two islands to work out their interlocking relationships in a satisfactory way. The problems, resolved elsewhere, have been pushed into this corner of Ireland where, it was hoped, they would be forgotten. The people of Northern Ireland, all of them, have been the victims.

We all need a new and generous vision. We need both to abandon the sterile exclusivity of "ourselves alone" and we need the positive encouragement of the third party—the British government. I believe that there are those in the Protestant community who have that wider vision, who cherish their Irishness and resent those who would narrow its definition to exclude them. I would appeal to such people to step forward now and present us with proposals for a new Ireland that is acceptable to Protestantism as opposed to unionism. Let them by so doing mount a positive challenge to those of my own tradition to meet the responsibility we have not yet measured up to, to spell out in clear and tangible terms what we mean by unity, what we mean by partnership, what we mean by reconciliation.

As for the British government, they have put peace in Ireland at the top of the agenda, the place where it should be, because it is the greatest human problem facing them. However, certain right-wing members of the Conservative Party backbenches constantly put obstacles in the way purely for internal party reasons. Their defence is that they are protecting the interests of the Unionist people. Are they? The bottom line of the British government's position is agreement among our divided people. Agreement threatens no section of our community. Would those backbenchers care to reflect on Winston Churchill's foresight in 1912 when he said in opposition to Bonar Law's support for the UVF's opposition to Home Rule and insistence on the Unionist veto: "Half a province cannot obstruct forever the reconciliation between the British and Irish peoples"? The peoples of both islands, particularly the people of Northern Ireland, have paid a terrible price for ignoring Churchill's advice.

The Unionists continue to refuse to reach agreement and rely on the British government and parliament to sustain the unacceptable status quo, instead of tackling the fundamental problem of agreement and persuading them to reach such agreement. Indeed, the ultimate guarantee to the Unionist people is to challenge them to recognise that they must trust themselves, stand on their own feet and for the first time reach an agreement that will protect forever their heritage and their tradition.

I am, however, encouraged by the commitment of the British and Irish governments to construct a framework whose objective is to accommodate a more positive relationship between our two peoples. Within that framework it is my hope that we can build a more positive, stable and lasting relationship among the people of this island. We can develop a new Ireland and a new relationship with Britain that will protect the vital interests of our major traditions—if we have the will to achieve it. Better to build such a framework than another wall in Belfast.

— 5 —

The Unionist Heritage

Ulster says "No".

Andrew Bonar Law

Ulster will fight and Ulster will be right!

Lord Randolph Spenser Churchill

In 1912 the British government introduced the third Home Rule Bill for Ireland. It was not independence but it was autonomy. The Unionists took up arms and the leader of the Conservative Party in Britain, Bonar Law, came to Belfast and spoke to a mass rally of the Ulster Volunteer Force (UVF), who were using violence in an attempt to sabotage the proposal for Home Rule. He told them that there were things stronger than parliamentary majorities. The government of the day backed down and unleashed events which a few years later led to the 1916 Easter Rising. Until then, there had been no support at all in Ireland for a violent approach. In fact, in the Easter Rising the support only came when the leaders were executed. In the 1918 election Sinn Féin won an overwhelming majority of the seats in Ireland. In that sense the Unionists created the 1916 reaction: the belief that the only thing the British understand is force.

I believe that not only then, but throughout the period of the existence of the southern state, Irish nationalism did not have a great understanding of the complexities of the North. It is only in the last twenty-five years that the real internal debate between the southern parties and ourselves has taken place. Until then it was a simplistic view—the Dáil, the Irish parliament, made a unanimous declaration in 1949, more or less saying, Brits out and unite Ireland. Republicans have been saying the same thing ever since, but nobody ever spelled out how they were going to achieve it.

Home Rule could have been the right stepping stone. If there had been Home Rule, then the evolutionary process would have continued. Gladstone said his greatest failure was not achieving Home Rule for Ireland, because, as he said, it would have been followed in time by Home Rule for England, Scotland and Wales. In the end, that would have led to a federation of the four, which would have been ideal. It would have mirrored the structure of the Europe of today long before it happened there. But the success of Unionist action in 1912 prevented Home Rule from being established and provided a model for similar actions every time it looked as if the British government was going to change things.

I ask the Unionist people, largely from the Protestant tradition, to re-examine their attitudes. The objective of the Unionist people—the preservation and protection of their identity, their ethos and their way of life—is a totally honourable and worthy objective with which no one can quarrel. My question to the Unionist people is not about their objective but about their methods.

It appears to me that the basic method used to achieve that objective has been for them to hold all power in their own hands. To include anyone else is seen as a threat and as ultimately leading to the undermining of the Unionist ethos: "What we have we hold, we do not share." It seems to me that such an attitude reveals a deep lack of self-confidence in themselves. This is underlined by what appears to be the persistent need for the British government to repeat their guarantee of the union. The fact that the ministers have to repeat it so regularly reveals a fundamental distrust of the commitment to the guarantee by British governments.

History confirms that distrust. Henry Grattan, one of the towering Protestant figures in Irish history, was guaranteed in 1782 that his parliament would last forever. Forever lasted eighteen years. The Church of Ireland was then guaranteed that it would remain the Established Church. That guarantee lasted a little longer: sixty-seven years. The sense of alienation in the Protestant community is based on a deep-seated distrust of such guarantees.

The real strength of the Unionist people rests in their own numbers, their deep conviction and their geography. This problem cannot be solved without their agreement, they are their own guarantors, and we will achieve lasting peace when their representatives stand on their own feet and negotiate an agreement with those other people with whom they share a piece of earth. Such an approach would be totally in keeping with my understanding of the basis of Protestantism—the acceptance of plurality—which has been so effectively practised by the Protestant tradition in so many countries across Europe where similar religious differences existed.

The Irish Protestant tradition has produced great and good people: Swift and Goldsmith will forever exemplify their talent, Grattan and Burke their altruism, and the American War of Independence, the American Constitution and as many as eleven American Presidents their abilities and their love of liberty. It is moreover the tradition which historically played the first and leading role in propounding libertarian values in Ireland.

Irish Protestants have always sought to maintain their distinctiveness and I admire and commend them for doing so. Yet, it seems to me that they have gone astray and put their own heritage at risk. Only look at the results today: unionism has boasted for generations that it is the protection of the Protestant identity and Protestant values, but in the vitriol and sectarian diatribes of the louder voice of contemporary unionism is there the slightest vestige of the fundamental Protestant values of civil and religious liberty? What has gone wrong?

Historically, as I see it, the central and consistent mistake of Irish Protestantism is exclusivity. It is an inherently destabilising factor in any society and it contains within itself all the seeds of communal disintegration and violence. It is, after all, essentially negative: a denial of liberty to others, rather than an assertion of its own liberty. Tragically, this exclusivism, which is simply another word for unionism, has come to represent in communal terms in our society the inversion of those values that Protestantism pre-eminently epitomises in world culture: freedom of conscience, liberty of the individual, civil and religious freedoms.

I do not believe, however, that this mistaken path was chosen consciously or strategically by the Irish Protestant tradition. Events showed the way and principal among them was the consistent encouragement given by centuries of British policy to maintain a separate and exclusive existence apart from the other tradition in Ireland. This was solidified by the decision in 1921 to establish a political entity in the north-east of this island based on a simple sectarian headcount which deliberately created a guaranteed system of sectarian majority rule in this part of Ireland. The majority in Northern Ireland were thus clearly encouraged by the guaranteed link with Britain to maintain and never to dilute their own solidity as the only available basis of their security.

Other more tragic events have since intervened: the immense suffering shared by both sides, the thousands of deaths and injuries, the collapse of our economy, the end of the hopes of our young people, the vision of our future dominated by a brick wall soon smeared by the pornography of hatred and triumphalism in two languages foreign to each other but both English. Irish Protestants and Irish Catholics have to take a new and different view of where our vital interests lie if we are to survive. After centuries of misconception and false illusions, it will be difficult and painful, but it must be done.

The Unionist Protestants of Northern Ireland are justly proud of their heritage and their contribution to the world. They number political leaders, field marshals, captains of industry and colonial governors among their great achievers. They see themselves as a pragmatic, hardheaded, sceptical, robust people, and there is much in their history to justify their view. They have shown a corresponding tendency to regard their Nationalist Catholic neighbours throughout the island as a more fanciful and less realistic race. There may be much in the history of the dispossession and enforced illiteracy of the Catholic community to give colour to that view.

History has changed the face and condition of Ireland, and these opinions have been overtaken by events. The south started from a platform of no industry and relatively primitive agriculture in 1921, while the north was the only part of Ireland seriously affected at that time by the Industrial Revolution. Now the south has caught up with and overtaken the north economically. Until recent years, northern industry was in decline and was for the most part owned by outsiders.

Northern Ireland has no sovereign voice in the world, nor, significantly, in the European Union. Unionists have watched with envy tinged with resentment as Dublin exercised the presidency of the Council of the European Union. Unionists are, furthermore, dismayed at the decline of Britain's greatness to a point where, most galling of all, London must now treat Dublin as an equal in the councils of Europe. A hardheaded people should logically draw the conclusion that an arrangement with the south is in its best interest. I have no doubt that they would do so now were the problem of Northern Ireland purely economic. Of course, it is not.

The Unionists are a majority in Northern Ireland, but their political behaviour there can only be understood if they are seen, as they feel themselves to be, as a threatened minority on the island of Ireland. Theirs are the politics of the besieged, harkening back to the embattled people in the Siege of Derry. This explains their stubborn refusal to share power with the minority in Northern Ireland, whom they fear as the Trojan horse of the "real" majority in Ireland, the Catholics. Hence, the similarity between their attitudes and, until recently, those of the whites of South Africa.

Can this attitude be unfrozen, as has been achieved in South Africa? There are some grounds for believing that it can. The main Unionist political group at the time of the Sunningdale experiment, and particularly its leader, the late Mr. Brian Faulkner, showed courage and political agility, and the response of most Unionists to the experiment was, by and large, benign. The pusillanimity of the Labour government in London, in failing to resist the predictable destructiveness of the demagogues and paramilitaries on the extremes of unionism, set back the situation almost irremediably; Unionist opinion, it must be admitted, shifted further to the right as a result, as evidenced by the electoral strength of Dr. Ian Paisley. Nevertheless, the reality of power-sharing did exist, however tenuously. Unionists, given the right leadership, were seen to be capable of magnanimity. We must move forward carefully but quickly now to benefit from the present opportunity for lasting peace. Unionist magnanimity must again take hold, this time more securely.

I am also encouraged by what I take to be a resurfacing of traditional Unionist realism. There is a growing suspicion among Unionists that their dependence on the British guarantee as the sole foundation of their political survival may in the long run be a risky and unprofitable enterprise. No leader of present mainline Unionist opinion has yet found the courage to put this squarely to his people, but several have expressed concern about the trustworthiness of the British.

My own Nationalist tradition has also failed to grasp the fundamental dimensions of our problems. We have failed to define our concept of unity in terms which would be meaningful and truly unthreatening to the other Irish tradition. Because of this fatal omission, our aspiration has by default come to mean and to be understood to mean: conquest. Unity and unity by agreement should be, if these words have any meaning, synonymous. This must mean the deliberate abjuring of conquest and triumphalism. Our failure in this matter—the result of misconceptions, weakness and illusion—has itself encouraged an extremism which perverts all the higher principles of our tradition.

Those who claim the right to kill and the right to die in the name of what they conceive to be Irish unity subvert not only the hope and meaning of unity but the integrity of their own tradition. When the most fundamental right, the right to live, is made subsidiary to a political principle, all other civic and religious values are diminished. Years ago, a murder would have filled whole pages of our newspapers; today it receives the passing comment merited by a squalid and routine misdemeanour. Other crimes are now so commonplace as not to receive any mention. Yet the suffering, the dislocation and the despair occasioned by all these tragedies are no less real now to those directly touched by them than they would have been years ago.

Now is the moment when political leaders in Northern Ireland, in the Republic and in Britain must radically re-examine their own fundamental assumptions. As I see it, the two greatest problems in Northern Ireland are the British guarantee, which inhibits such re-examination, and the Unionist dependence on it. Given economic developments in the Republic, and the growing suspicion about Britain's long-term intentions on the part of many Unionists, this is a crucial juncture at which to pursue serious initiative. Britain can create the conditions in which Unionists can perceive and pursue their true interests.

I believe that the true interests of Unionists depend precisely on the exercise of their traditional gifts of self-confidence and self-reliance. The time has come for them to believe in themselves as their own guarantors in a future shared with the other people of the island of Ireland.

As it is now, Unionists see themselves as a threatened minority on the island of Ireland. If you ask a Unionist how real the threat is, he or she will tell you of friends or relatives who have been murdered or injured by the Provisional IRA. That, however, is only a vivid and chilling expression of an even deeper sense of intimidation. Unionists fear that they would be culturally and racially overwhelmed by the Catholic Nationalist majority if they were to join with the rest of the island. But would they? This is the challenge to Irish nationalism, to Dublin, to the Nationalist minority in Northern Ireland, and to the friends of Irish nationalism around the world.

The time has come for London and Dublin to make it clear that there are no longer any unconditional guarantees for any section of the Northern community. There is only a commitment to achieving a situation in which there are guarantees for all. They should make it clear that there is in fact no easy solution, but only a process that will lead to a solution, and they should declare themselves committed to such a process.

Indeed, on embarking on this process Unionists ought to be encouraged by the example of both the United States and the European Union. In the United States, in spite of deep differences of origin and background, a constitution has been formed which is able to harness great differences for the common good. Yet the Italians remain Italian, African-Americans are still African-American, and the Irish still parade on St. Patrick's Day. They have created a unity in diversity.

Europe itself has suffered centuries of bloody conflict. In this century alone, the peoples of Europe have been locked in the savagery of two world wars with a bitterness and slaughter that go far beyond anything that we have experienced on this island. Yet, fifty years after World War II, as a result of an agreed process, they have been able to create one parliament to represent them, one community—and the Germans are still Germans, the French are still French. They have a unity in diversity.

Is it too much to ask that we on this small island do precisely the same thing? Is it too much to ask that these two responsible governments declare themselves now in favour of such a process? Can we too build a unity in diversity?

I was in Berlin a week after the Berlin Wall fell, a moment of great hope right across Europe. But I was conscious that, as the Berlin Wall was falling, the Belfast walls were rising. I made a speech in Berlin in the Reichstag at that time about that very subject. I brought with me a piece of the Belfast wall and presented it to Willy Brandt. The walls are an indictment of us all because we created them; they were built by our past attitudes. The positive way to look at them is as a challenge, that unless we all re-examine our past attitudes, we will not bring the walls down. This means, in effect, that each mind-set that has built those walls has to re-examine itself.

The re-examination cannot take place until the Nationalist mind-set recognises that it is people who have rights, not territory. The Unionist mind-set, which is "we are a minority in Ireland, so to protect ourselves we must hold all power in our hands and exclude everyone else", leads to widespread discrimination and conflict. Both mind-sets have to change to recognise that when you share a piece of earth with other people, the only way to do so is by consensus.

Ireland's problems are not unique in European or world history. Many countries have backgrounds of historical national conflict, tensions with neighbouring states and internal differences of language, religion or national identity. The lesson learned by many of these countries was that difference of itself need not be a problem. The issue for those seeking stability and harmony was not the elimination of diversity but its accommodation. They learned that there was no peace, no stability, no security in seeking to have political arrangements which reflected and respected only one tradition and its values. Stability, and the best protection for any tradition, lay in creating a political consensus with structures which neither privileged nor prejudiced the position of any tradition.

When we look at the United States of America and see a country of broad and deep differences protected by a political consensus, it is ironic to realise that people from the Irish Protestant tradition helped to fashion the Declaration of Independence, the Constitution and the Bill of Rights. They helped set in place, in that new country, democracy and the essence of real unity—the acceptance of diversity. It is a lesson that they had doubtless learned from the Ireland they left behind them. It was a lesson that they shared with the other groups who helped to found and fashion the United States with them and who had come from elsewhere in Europe, having left societies in which there was intolerance, injustice and a rampant abuse of power.

In recognising the importance of their contribution to the understanding and operation of democracy we see the real Protestant heritage in politics. Other European countries which embrace societies of difference all give testimony to the positive Protestant contribution to the creation of political structures based on pluralism. The Protestant heritage in Europe and in America was not to seek political structures or societies made in their own image. Rather than proceed with the negative motivation of suspicion and mistrust of others, often well-grounded, they harnessed the positive motivation of self-confidence in their talents and their values.

Unfortunately, this openness is not part of the Protestant heritage in Ireland, evident in the continual use of the negative—"Ulster Says No", "No Surrender", "Not an Inch". The approach of Protestant Unionist leaders in Ireland has been to turn difference into divisions, to create separation rather than accommodation, and to have all power in their own hands. That approach has failed the Protestant Unionist community just as it has offended the Catholic Nationalist tradition.

Nationalists in Ireland must properly ask themselves why nationalism has not been fulfilled in Ireland as it was in other countries throughout Europe. The nationalism which united those other countries included that spirit of tolerance and active pluralism which has served to accommodate difference. Their nationalism sought more to unite than to assimilate or vindicate. In Ireland, Nationalists, understandably, given a history of colonisation and ascendancy, fell into the trap of identification with mainly one tradition. In doing so they were diverted from the real republicanism of pluralism, tolerance and democracy which ironically was first, and perhaps best, articulated by members of Protestant denominations in Ireland.

It is sadly true that this distortion of real republicanism was made more savage by the hurt suffered by people in the Nationalist tradition through repression, partition and discrimination. This resulted in some of the Nationalist community turning to violence and so worsening the divisions and condition of our country and its people.

It is fair to say, however, that others from the Nationalist tradition want to erase that grotesque caricature of republicanism which is violent and sectarian. We have sought to come to generous and realistic terms with the rights and needs of those in Ireland who feel offended or threatened by Nationalist Ireland as it has been understood, or misunderstood, for too long. We have much more to do in terms of understanding through dialogue and co-operation, achieving not assimilation but reconciliation. That would give us real Irish unity—the unity of the Irish people giving expression to the positive diversity of our people.

Unfortunately, representatives of the Unionist tradition have refused to engage in such a process of reconciliation.

They have opposed measures aimed at achieving equality in Northern Ireland. We cannot have real reconciliation in circumstances where we do not have equality. The political role of the British has been to allow the suspicions, self-doubts and prejudices of Unionists to dictate the boundaries of political change in Ireland and to restrict the development of relations between Britain and Ireland.

— 6 —

Attitudes in the Irish Republic

Now and in time to be, wherever green is worn,
Things are changed, changed utterly:
A terrible beauty is born.

William Butler Yeats

Whatever arguments, criticisms or refinements one might discuss about the 1937 Constitution of the Republic of Ireland, it did give the people of the twenty-six counties the basis for a very peaceful and stable society. This is something which the people of the North have never had, largely because the North has never really had a constitution, in spite of the fact that every election there since 1920 was fought "on the constitution". What purported to be a constitution or system of government never addressed one of the basic functions of a constitution, which is to accommodate difference and diversity. It is again worth remembering that Irish Presbyterians, people whose immediate past memory was that they had been driven from Ireland by religious intolerance, had significant input in drafting the Constitution of the United States. It is not surprising therefore that the central principle of that constitution was the recognition that the essence of unity was the acceptance of diversity—*e pluribus unum.*

That is the central principle which has given peace and stability to every democratic state in the world today and it is a tragedy that, although its acceptance in the US Constitution was heavily influenced by the experiences of Irish people mainly from the Presbyterian tradition, it is a principle which has never really been put into practice in Ireland itself, and certainly not by Ulster Protestants. The challenge to all of us for the future is whether or not that principle is going to be both accepted and implemented. Without it there will be no peace or stability and we will continue as we have done in the past—not to accept difference but to push it to the point of division, with all its tragic consequences. That challenge faces us starkly on the streets of the North. What has happened there is a result of our failure, and the failure of all of those involved, to accommodate our differences.

The challenge is particularly relevant to unionism. It is hardly unfair to say that unionism in Northern Ireland has never been about the accommodation of difference. It has been about maintaining it. Indeed, there has never been the slightest acknowledgement that we live in a divided society, or that there was any need to accommodate difference. Unionism has always been an oligarchy based on sectarian solidarity and any time that oligarchy was threatened by British proposals for greater accommodation, the response was consistent and simple—threaten dire consequences.

Successive British governments have backed down in the face of Unionist threats. A serious consequence of this was that Unionist leadership remained in the hands of those who were uncompromising and any dissenting voices got very little hearing. Another consequence was that it gave justification to those in the Nationalist community who argue that the British only understand force. This vicious circle of threats of force and actual force has paralysed all political development in the northern part of Ireland and is, indeed, the real "Irish problem".

The Irish government and most Nationalists in Ireland have repeatedly given convincing evidence of their repudiation of the violence of the Provisionals—the public by its consistent rejection at the polls of those who support violence, and the Irish government by its active pursuit of the people of violence, its commitment of additional police and army units to the border areas, and the introduction of draconian legal measures to secure convictions in the courts. Dublin and Irish opinion generally clearly intend no threat to Unionists; on the contrary, the leaders of Irish-American opinion, which was often seen by Unionists to be hostile to their interests and supportive of violence, have in recent years repeatedly condemned support for violence from the United States. This has had the double effect of reducing material assistance for the Provisional IRA from the United States and of going some way toward assuaging one source of Unionist anxiety.

Despite these positive elements, there is an important sense in which the Dublin government has not yet fully clarified its intentions.

The southern state is seen by many Unionists (in varying degrees by the majority) as a lay expression of sectarian Catholic values. As such, it is unacceptable to them. The reality, as I encounter it, is that the Republic is a modern state struggling to develop its economy and society within a European framework. The partition of Ireland, seventy-five years ago, created a state in the south with an overwhelmingly Catholic population. Inevitably, Catholic values were enshrined in some areas of law, particularly family law. Unionists have a right to be convinced that the south is serious when it declares its intention to embody pluralist values in the law of the united Ireland to which it aspires. Until recently, the evidence for these intentions has been inadequate.

Even more seriously, Nationalist statements which contain hints of irredentism, of conquest, of compulsion, do not promote a policy of unity; moreover, they give comfort to those who believe in violence. The Irish government repudiates violence and by its actions is seen to do so. It should, nevertheless, in claiming the ground of nationalism, clarify, if necessary *ad nauseam*, its commitment to unity by agreement, only by agreement, and through reconciliation.

Since the beginning of the civil rights movement in the North and the changes initiated by it, Articles Two and Three of the 1937 Constitution have come under particular scrutiny and have been represented by Unionists in particular as asserting some sort of imperialist claim over the North. I regard them somewhat differently, and again we must underline that this Constitution was drafted against the background of 1937 attitudes. What is important in the current context is that those two articles did exactly as their author intended. They asserted the sovereignty of the Irish people—an assertion that was clearly necessary at that time—while at the same time subtly affirming that that sovereignty was not complete, that there was division within Ireland about its exercise and application. This was done by making clear that the jurisdiction of the Constitution did not apply in practice or in reality to the North of Ireland. It was further confirmed by the fact that only the population of the twenty-six counties was asked to vote on it.

If today Irish Nationalists can face up to the reality of division over sovereignty, we open up the possibility of real answers. We have no shortage in this century, particularly in politics, of masters of rhetoric or sloganeers asserting with hand on heart and with all the emotional fervour at their command the right of the Irish people to self-determination or, as the more self-righteous put it, the indefensible right of the Irish people to sovereignty. Such people conveniently forget, or ignore, the fact that the people of Ireland are divided as to how those rights should be implemented or exercised.

Of course the Irish people have a right to self-determination. Of course the Irish people have a right to sovereignty. But what we have to recognise specifically, and not set aside or ignore, is the central fact that the people of Ireland are divided as to how that sovereignty should be exercised or how that self-determination should be expressed. And by the Irish people I mean all of the people who live in this island.

It is the search for agreement among the Irish people as to how to express that self-determination or how to exercise that sovereignty that is the major challenge facing those in Ireland today who wish to achieve the unity of the people of Ireland within an independent republic. The search for such agreement is the real search for peace and stability. It is a search that has been with us since Wolfe Tone first asserted it, but which has never been faced up to in any serious or sustained way. It has instead been replaced with rhetoric or verbal republicanism. It is surely also self-evident that it is a search that cannot possibly be pursued by force, for even if victory by force were possible its results are only conquest and humiliation, no basis for a stable future. Indeed it is surely by now self-evident that force in a divided society only drives people further apart.

The healing of the divisions between Catholic and Protestant in Ireland, however difficult that may be, is the major challenge and the major priority facing those who wish to exercise the self-determination of all the Irish people and establish permanent peace in Ireland.

There is now widespread agreement in Britain, as well as in Ireland, that the future of Ireland can only be determined by the people of Ireland themselves, north and south. Article One of the 1985 Anglo-Irish Agreement spelled that out, and it is also the basis of the 1993 Downing Street Declaration. No doubt there will be voices declaring that no minority has the right to frustrate the will of the majority, a view which has a certain ideological rectitude. However, the factual rectitude is that no major decisions can be taken about the future of the people in the North without the agreement of the Northern Protestant population, due to its numbers and its concentration in a geographical area of this island.

Can anyone really visualise the unity of the Irish people without the agreement of both sections of the community?

The acknowledgement of that fact by all who claim to be Nationalist or Republican will in itself be a major step in breaking down the barriers between us, because it will give confidence to the Protestant people of the North that conquest of them or destruction of their ethos forms no part of our dialogue. If that dialogue could take place in such an atmosphere of genuine mutual respect, it would have a much better chance of really breaking down the barriers between us.

More significantly, of course, the same Article One of the Anglo-Irish Agreement made clear that, in the event of such agreement, the British government will both accept it and facilitate it. This has been restated in the Downing Street Declaration.

Are we not now challenged to begin seriously the search for agreement among Catholic, Protestant and Dissenter on the issue of self-determination?

The search for such agreement has yet to be seriously undertaken. Those who were engaged in an armed struggle laid down their weapons for seventeen months in order to join with the rest of us, for the first time in history, in a massive effort to achieve such agreement. With a restoration of the ceasefire and continued commitment to an agreement which must earn the allegiance of all our traditions, would the Unionist people not see such an effort as a major gesture of goodwill and commitment to real peace and real agreement on this island? It goes without saying that the central principle of that agreement, a principle first expressed by Irish Presbyterians in the eighteenth century, would be that the essence of our unity must be the acceptance of our diversity.

— 7 —

Violence: An Indictment of Everyone

This contest is one of endurance and it is not those who can inflict most, but they who can suffer most, who will conquer.

Terence MacSwiney

The campaign of violence of the Provisional IRA set back and distorted the cause of Irish nationalism in the eyes of Unionists, and of British and world opinion. It is clear that a majority of the people in Ireland as a whole, including a majority of Catholics in Northern Ireland, both favour Irish unity as a solution and reject violence as a means of promoting that solution.

Until their 1994 ceasefire, the Provisionals were relatively impervious to the universal rejection of their methods for a number of reasons. Firstly, they were sustained by an extremely simple view of the Irish problem, and in this simplicity they found strength and purpose. For the Provisionals, the Irish problem consisted of the British presence in Ireland—nothing more. Remove that presence, they claimed, and the problem would quickly be solved by the establishment of a unified, independent Irish state. This analysis of things afforded a simplistic view of a highly complex situation. It also provided the inspiration for violent action resulting from its clear affinities with the vision of the partially successful and widely revered insurgents of the 1916–23 period. They, in their determination to secure freedom for the greater part of the Irish people, were understandably distracted from the peculiar circumstances which obtained in the six north-eastern counties of Ulster.

A second factor in Provisional endurance was the encouragement which they—like the Loyalist extremists—were able to draw from British weakness and prevarication.

Thirdly, I believe that the case for Irish nationalism has not been clearly enough expounded by Irish Nationalist leaders. The Provisionals did not hesitate to exploit the ambiguities of policy and the innuendoes of the public debate to seek to claim support of, or justification for, their actions.

Fourthly, unjustifiable excesses by British security forces, condemned by the European Court of Human Rights as inhuman and degrading, created an implacable hostility to Britain in the minds of many who were subjected to them. These excesses, together with the introduction of internment without trial in 1971, long since abandoned, did more to gain recruits for the Provisionals than any exhortations to "blood sacrifice" from the patriarchs of the movement.

Fifthly, the absence of political activity from the life of Northern Ireland provided both an opportunity and an argument to the people of violence: they could, with some credibility, play upon the frustrations of the minority in the absence of political hope and ask, in the face of British immobilism: Who but we are doing anything about Northern Ireland?

Finally, it could be seen for some time that the Provisionals had hardened into a ruthless force which compensated in terms of experience and technique for what it lost in political support. A long time ago, commentators invoked Mao and predicted that, as the water of popular approval dried up, the guerilla fish would have to abandon the struggle to survive. We saw that the fish needed less water than we had thought. The Provisionals for several years received only insignificant support from the population of either

Northern Ireland or the Republic, yet they retained the ability to disrupt.

Indeed, their activities descended to a level of savagery which all but numbed the capacity of the public to respond with horror to their inhuman atrocities. Life became cheap—and the entire community to some extent dehumanised. "Is there a life before death?" asks a piece of anonymous graffiti on a Belfast wall. The writer might also have asked whether there is any childhood left for the battle-scarred children of the ghettos of that city, and of the rest of Northern Ireland.

Aside from the immorality of its actions, the Provisional IRA campaign of violence had no hope of success. It is, I suppose, conceivable that it might have eventually frightened a feeble British government out of Northern Ireland. What would almost certainly have followed would have been a bloodbath. This would quickly spread to the south, and, after thousands of deaths, would have finally resolved itself by the division of the island into two bristling, homogeneous sectarian states, neither stable, both sunk in the obscurantism of their most extreme supporters. It is not possible for a political settlement to result from a military victory in Northern Ireland, whether by the Provisionals, the Loyalists or the British government.

The Provisional IRA have often been dismissed as mindless, as criminals, as gangsters. I do not dismiss them as such. I believe, in spite of my profound disagreement with and unequivocal condemnation of their methods, that they actually believe in what they have done. That is why I entertained the hope that sooner rather than later they would respond to the unanswerable case that exists against their campaign, and transfer their considerable energies and organisation to totally peaceful means of achieving their political objectives.

They might reflect that, during their twenty-five-year-old campaign, their so-called "mistakes"—one of the worst of which was the bombing of a war memorial service in

Enniskillen—were not in fact exceptions, but were direct consequences of the very nature of their campaign and because of that, irrespective of other arguments, rendered their campaign totally unjustifiable. Fifty-five per cent of all people who died in the Troubles in the North were innocent civilians—people killed by "mistake", or in tit-for-tat revenge killings by Loyalist paramilitaries. It was clear, therefore, that at least one of every two people who died was totally innocent, because that was the pattern that derived from the very nature of their campaign. There could be no justification in statements of regret or apology, because they knew in advance that that was specifically what would happen.

For many years they defended their actions by regretting that accidents always happen in war. Leaving aside the fact that they had no right to declare war, if that were true then one might expect to witness equal numbers of "mistakes" or accidents on all sides. The facts are that twelve per cent of all civilians were killed by the security forces (the British army, the Royal Ulster Constabulary (RUC) and the Ulster Defence Regiment (UDR) put together) and eighty-seven per cent by Nationalist and Loyalist paramilitaries. Look even at their own fatalities, their own members who lost their lives. Of 279 Nationalist paramilitaries who lost their lives, 117 were killed by the security forces, 20 by Loyalists and 142 by themselves, either in "accidents" or "executions". More than one out of two Nationalist paramilitaries who lost their lives, did so at their own hands.

By any standards, even military standards, how could any such campaign be justified, particularly in the name of patriotism or of an Ireland whose people overwhelmingly disapproved of such a campaign? Was there a single injustice in Northern Ireland that justified the taking of a human life? The leadership necessary, given the nature of the IRA, did not have the moral courage to admit that they should abandon what they called "armed struggle". If they needed Republican precedents for their actions, they had but to remember Pádraig Pearse, who once issued a statement calling on his followers to lay down their arms lest they bring too much suffering on their own people.

Are there any such people in the Provisional IRA? It appears that there are, for they had the moral courage to declare a major ceasefire. No single act in this century has done more to transform the atmosphere on this island, and to begin the process of breaking down the barriers between our people which are the real problem on this island today and which are the real legacy of our past, barriers which were intensified by the IRA campaign of violence. The ceasefire must be restored.

Let us now turn to the political reasons given by the Provisional IRA for their campaign—reasons which they declared to be their sole driving force and therefore reasons which should be examined seriously in any discussion of their campaign. The main reason given by the IRA for their campaign is that Britain is in Ireland to defend her own interests, by force, those interests being economic and military. Is there anyone today who seriously believes that Britain is in Northern Ireland defending economic interests? Does anyone in modern nuclear Europe really believe that Britain has a strategic interest in a military presence in Ireland? The reasons no longer exist. The fundamental nature of British–Irish relationships has changed in today's new Europe. By abandoning violence, the IRA showed that they were serious about their political objectives.

The British–Irish quarrel is European in its origins. It is often forgotten that Ireland's close links with Europe over the centuries were the fundamental reason for England's involvement in Ireland. The Plantation of Ulster was England's response to the clan chieftains, O'Neill and O'Donnell, and their links with Spain. The Act of Union of 1800 was England's response to the French revolutionary invasion of Ireland under the republican banner of Wolfe Tone. Even the Royal College of St. Patrick at Maynooth was set up in 1795 because of England's fear of the influences of the Irish colleges in Rome, Paris, Salamanca and Louvain. England saw Ireland as the back door for her European enemies and moved into Ireland to defend her own interests, with all the serious consequences for the Irish people.

All that has now changed and both Ireland and Britain are members of the European Union and both its peoples have voted in referenda for such membership. Ireland is rebuilding her links with other European countries and, indeed, is well placed to become part of the European majority. It is quite clear, therefore, that no one could argue that Britain is in Ireland today defending either military or economic interests. Issues like independence and sovereignty, issues at the heart of the British–Irish quarrel, have changed their meaning in the new Europe because we now have interdependence and shared sovereignty.

Nonetheless, a serious legacy remains. We have a very deeply divided people on this island. That is the major problem facing us today and it is clear that the healing of these divisions would be much more easily achieved with the co-operation and goodwill of Britain. It is clear, too, that membership of the European Union and the lessons of that community are major factors that can assist in the required healing process.

If both parts of Ireland can enter into new relationships with Greeks, Italians, French, Germans, and all the others, it is surely long past time when they should be forging new relationships with one another. If bitter enemies like France and Germany can build new relationships, can we not do the same?

If someone had stood up fifty years ago, when tens of millions of people, not for the first time in this century, had been slaughtered and cities devastated, and said that we would have a united Europe and the French would still be French and the Germans would still be German, that person would have been described as a fool or a dreamer. Thank

God we did have people of vision, and surely we can apply exactly the same lessons and methods to our problem in Ireland. But how?

Let the British and Irish governments together follow the example of the European Union. Let them make a joint declaration that the divisions among the people of Ireland and the prejudices that are at their root are the regrettable consequences of our history and are not in the best interests of the people of Ireland or of the European Union; that the two governments have decided to leave the past aside; that they have decided to build institutions in Ireland, north and south, which will respect difference but which will allow the people in both parts of Ireland to work their common ground, together. This common ground, largely economic, is already considerable and will become even more considerable if the IRA ceasefire is reinstated. Indeed, with the removal of commercial borders and the creation of the channel tunnel, that common ground and economic interest will intensify as we become the offshore island of a united Europe.

For centuries, the peoples of Western Europe slaughtered one another; their historical legacy was far more bitter than ours. They have shown that they can build common institutions which preserve their differences, which allow them to work their common economic ground together. They continue to grow together towards a unity whose form is agreed by all and whose essence is the acceptance of diversity. Can we not do the same on this small island?

Let the IRA lay down their arms forever, and let them join everyone else in the real task of breaking down those barriers in our hearts and minds, in tackling the human problems of economic deprivation, which is what politics is really about—the right to a decent existence for all our people in our own land.

For the first time in seventy years, the energies and talents of all Irish people at home and abroad, including the enormous political clout of our friends in the United States and Europe, are at our disposal. The challenge to the IRA remains—is your philosophy in the genuine Republican tradition of Tone, striving to unite Catholic, Protestant and Dissenter, which clearly can never be done by force, or is it in the territorial tradition of the Defenders, a tradition of no hope?

Part Four

Ireland at Peace

— 8 —

Politics Alone

Put up what flags you like,
It is too late to save your soul with bunting.
Louis MacNeice

Throughout the twenty-five-year period of violence, and especially in the early eighties in the stalemate after the deaths of the hunger-strikers, there was no disguising the bleakness of the scene that confronted us in Northern Ireland. It confronted not just the SDLP, but the entire community. In every sphere of life, whether it was politics, security, or the economy, the outlook was grim. The challenge to us therefore was great, but we had been facing challenges since our foundation in 1970. My mother used to say, "If you are reared in your bare feet, you will never get pneumonia in the snow." The SDLP had been in their political bare feet since the start. When the snows and the storms of conflict came, we did not get pneumonia, but we met the challenge and sought to overcome.

They said that we had an economic crisis. But had we an economy? The numbers of unemployed outstripped those in the manufacturing industry, our traditional industry—once the symbol of unionism's so-called sturdy resilience. Our new industries were either shrinking or departed. There was no new investment. The spreading economic Sahara—symbolised by Strabane, Dungannon and Newry, with half of their menfolk on the dole—had engulfed us all. Because this community had not gathered its courage, because we had failed to share power, we had condemned ourselves to share poverty.

Meanwhile, violence thrived. The IRA and INLA competed with each other in the league tables of cruelty. The security forces, or a section of them, persisted in their attempts to bend the law and succeeded only in adding to the toll of deaths, lending sick justification to the people of violence. Loyalist extremists would not be left out of this test of manhood. Urged on relentlessly by ambitious, perverted, bigoted demagogues and by the ever-sounding bugle in the blood, they murdered the innocent and armed for the showdown.

Politics, our only hope, were never bleaker. The British government was dominated by someone who seemed to care little about the problem of Northern Ireland. Northern Ireland, Mrs. Thatcher said, was as British as Finchley. We hoped, at least for the sake of Finchley, that she was wrong. James Prior's Northern Ireland Assembly was, we were told, a major government initiative. Yet she did not mention it when she visited Northern Ireland or indeed anywhere else. We were again, what we have so often been for British politicians: either an embarrassing nuisance to be concealed from view if possible, or a political football in which our fortunes were usually neglected.

On the ground, political deadlock showed no signs of decongealing. Our opponents outdid each other in intransigence and bigotry. In Mr. Prior's Assembly, we were regularly presented with the unedifying spectacle of adults slugging it out over arcane disputes which amounted to literally nothing. In the black circumstances of Northern Ireland, this could only be described as the most irresponsible show on earth.

Our community was in a dangerous plight. Justice and humanity demanded that all men and women of goodwill should cry out for a solution, but this had not happened. The SDLP had to make it happen—and we had to succeed.

Again and again, we had to insist that there was only one way forward: the peaceful and constitutional way. This way did not kill, it did not destroy, it did not coerce, it did not intimidate, it did not impoverish. Unlike violence, it could succeed. What had the violence of those years achieved, what had it created, besides hatred, despair and grief? I attempted to sum up the real achievements of the Provisionals, as seen by ourselves:

> We also see in those parts of the community where the Provisional IRA are more active, the spread of a foul social cancer. The cohesion of society, at the best of times, is both deep-rooted and fragile. Its roots—the shared principles of respect for life, liberty and order—can go deep, but they must be tended and watered assiduously and incessantly. There are now communities in Northern Ireland where these roots have not alone been neglected, but have been hacked away and poisoned by the Provisional IRA's campaign against the fundamental human right to live until God calls us. What has followed is a gross distortion of moral values in society, the promotion of the pornography of death and nihilism on our gable walls, and the deep corruption of the young.

The Provisionals sought support at the ballot box for their campaign. They had some measure of success. Not a vote for violence, some said, but the result of frustration, resentment and the negative nature of the Assembly election—a protest vote. Maybe so.

A vote for these people was—and these were their own words—a vote for "unambivalent support for the armed struggle". Translated into the reality of the streets, that was a vote for killing industrialists and destroying investment in a community starved of work. It was a vote for killing working men and women in the Protestant community who had donned uniforms and who saw themselves, no matter how we or anyone else saw them, as the defenders of the Protestant tradition and way of life in this island. It was a vote for the murder of public figures as they left their place of worship, striking at religious traditions that were deep and dear to the people of this country. It was a vote to justify the planting of bombs in places of entertainment, classified as "legitimate" targets, and the killing and maiming of the innocent. It was the use of the ballot paper to encourage the young to use the Armalite and to spend the best years of their lives behind prison walls.

Apart from graves, mangled bodies, overpopulated prisons and lengthening dole queues, what did this policy of armed struggle achieve? Perhaps those who advocated it would tell us. Perhaps they would tell the young people whom they sought to attract to their ranks.

We asked these questions. We confronted them in every single constituency. We wanted to hear—not more lies about two wrongs making a right, not more use of one atrocity to justify another, not an endless list of "what abouts". We wanted to know in what way the killing had advanced the reconciliation and unity of the people of Ireland. We even wanted to know how it could cure the dampness in Rossville Flats or the desperate living conditions of the people of Moyard. We wanted to know how it could give hope to our unemployed and in particular to our young.

The SDLP have never been a flag-waving party. We do not play on people's emotions. Our record in exposing injustice in Northern Ireland is clear and unequivocal. Our record in exposing and opposing the dispensers of death, whether it be the excesses of security forces or the planned murders of paramilitaries, is writ for all to see. Our commitment to non-violence is unflinching because it is right.

Our alternative is neither dramatic nor romantic—we offer politics alone as the path to peace. Politics is about the reconciliation of difference—one of the most noble tasks facing this world today in the many theatres of conflict that threaten to engulf us.

We offer patient political negotiation. It is undramatic, unspectacular. As I have often said, patient political effort will not fill graves or jails. Violence will. Patient political effort will not lengthen a dole queue. Violence will. Patient political and non-violent effort has in fact brought about the only real achievements and benefits that we can claim over the past twenty-five years.

In 1983, we had not yet received any help from the people who bore responsibility for our nightmare, namely the British government. They were, after all, the government of Northern Ireland, with full power and responsibility. We were the victims, not of mere neglect, but of conscious and malevolent contempt. There was in the United Kingdom no other problem of comparable urgency, yet there was no evidence of any serious thinking by the government. Secretary of State after Secretary of State chose the softest option—Pontius Pilate's "Let them sort it out for themselves"—refusing to intervene among the mortals of Ireland.

What we were asking for from the British government, and what everyone in this bitter land had a right to expect from the British government, were wisdom and courage. Their basic policy—maintenance of the Unionist veto—had manifestly been a disaster, to be maintained only for irrational, triumphalist and self-defeating reasons.

For the truth was that the British government had no policy on Northern Ireland. There had been an abject failure to face up to the causes of the problem, to engage the principal parties to the conflict in realistic negotiation about the future, to identify British interests, or to develop a purposeful government strategy for solving the problem. If there was a strategy, what and where was it? This failure had led to the deadly impasse which paralysed us for so long, the net result being to embroil Britain in a long-term military commitment in which she had no vital interest commensurate with the expenditure of money and lives involved.

In the absence of a policy, British governments had fallen back upon a sterile unthinking reinforcement of the status quo, the traditional reflex of an imperial power in decline, a power which had lost interest and lost any sense of purpose in the maintenance of dominion. In the Northern Ireland context, that meant that to treat the problem in a wider context would have led to accusations of threatening the identity of the Unionist population. Thus had one, relatively small, lobby gained a stranglehold over government. Thus had government allowed itself to be trapped in a situation where Unionists needed only to refuse to negotiate to paralyse all of us.

When the SDLP asked the British to change the basis of their policy we were accused of the "coercion" of Unionists. If this charge had been true it would have appeared that our accusers took no exception to the fact that the maintenance of the present basis of policy had amounted to coercion of the Northern minority for the past seventy-five years, with dire human consequences. We were of course not asking that anyone be coerced. We were asking that the British government would set a new objective of policy and that they would begin the process of persuading everyone that this objective was to everyone's benefit. Was that not what all governments and political parties did when they produced a policy that they believed to be beneficial to society as a whole but with which some people disagreed? Would any political change ever take place if opposition to it by a substantial number of people at the outset led to its abandonment and that to persuade them otherwise was "coercion"? This would be absurd.

Reinforcing the identity of one section of the community while ignoring the other was coercion of the other. It begot alienation. Alienation begot violence. Violence begot repression and repression begot violence. This whole vicious circle, familiar throughout the history of our island, had to be broken. And it had to be broken by challenging the assumption which was the cornerstone of all British policy—that any settlement in the wider Irish framework threatened the fundamental interests of the Unionist community.

As for the Unionists themselves, they had become a petty people. They represented themselves as the defenders and protectors of the Protestant heritage in Ireland. No one had done more to destroy it. "Ourselves alone" was their motto. "Let us hold all power in our own hands" was their agenda. Exclusivism. Such a violating attitude could not harbour any trace of the civil and religious liberty that was their proud heritage and which was such a necessary first principle for any solution to the problems of Ireland.

It was a devastating commentary on their commitment to peace and stability that not once in the previous seventy-five years, and in particular not once in the previous bloody decade, had they produced a single new idea, a single new proposal. Where else in the world would a powerful and influential government, such as the British, have tied the whole basis of their policy to such a pathetic and leaderless bunch of politicians, who did not even accept the legitimacy of the Northern Ireland state which had been created for them? Their only legitimacy was themselves alone. Did anyone need to look any further for the roots of violence?

The assumption which underlies Unionist fear and which paralyses movement is that they cannot trust the rest of this island to guarantee their civil and religious liberty. That fundamental assumption had to be challenged and challenged effectively.

I genuinely believed that it was in the interests of this whole island that the majority population in the North be given the opportunity to consider a settlement soon, rather than in a more tense situation as the population distribution between majority and minority narrowed and reversed.

Armed with a blueprint for our new Ireland, which patently demonstrated that all interests were protected, we felt justified in asking for a change of British policy and a commitment from them, together with everyone else, to a campaign of persuasion of all those who still remained doubtful. That was the political road towards a new Ireland.

Firstly, of course, we would have to convince our fellow democrats south of the border. The SDLP held a memorable conference in 1983 to commemorate the bicentenary of Henry Grattan's parliament. On that occasion, the Taoiseach Dr. Garret FitzGerald, who was dedicated to resolving our conflict, said:

> The key to progress thus lies in the hands of the Nationalist people of this island, north and south, through the power, if they are prepared to exercise it, to dispel the legitimate fears of Northern Unionists and to remove the most crucial obstacle to fresh thinking about political structures in this island. The ball is at our feet in Dublin and Northern Nationalists have the capacity to influence us to play the game, if they commit themselves to demanding action from the people of the Irish state.

We agreed. And we sought that action. In proposing the setting up of a Council for a new Ireland, where all constitutional politicians committed to a new Ireland would define what we really wished this Ireland to be, the SDLP was doing no more than asking the democratic parties of the Republic to join with us in challenging British and Unionist unwillingness to change, and in preparing the way to meaningful dialogue with both.

I remain convinced that the difficult process of examining the obstacles in the way of a new Ireland would force those parties and ourselves to take many painful decisions—about the definition of Irishness, about the economic implications of unity by consent, about church–state relations, about British–Irish relations—decisions which they would ordinarily have preferred to avoid and which they had not been forced to consider at any time in the past.

In proposing this decision-making process, the SDLP was concerned primarily with defining and securing the rights of those who often, for good historical reasons, took refuge in the embattled past rather than face the contemporary frightening reality. This meant that democrats in the south and in the SDLP had to find the humility to acknowledge that we had so far failed to define an Irish identity which adequately accommodated all the traditions of this island. Our failure—an intellectual and a moral failure—had unwittingly created one of the principal inspirations of violence.

Every day that young people killed in the name of "Ireland", their acts of murder reinforced that narrow definition of Ireland which they and so many others had unquestioningly inherited, an "Ireland" defined in narrow and exclusive terms, together with a fanatical hatred of Britain, an "Ireland" which existed only in the minds of those who spoke of it, who killed for it and who died for it, but which bore no relation to the real Ireland, with its rich diversity of traditions and culture. We had for too long stressed this essential unity of Ireland but forgotten about its equally essential diversity. It was this failure to marry both and give them institutional expression that had been the failure of successive generations to solve the Irish problem.

There was no inherited wisdom in this matter. Young and old, we had to be ready to question our own inherited assumptions about ourselves, painfully, vigorously, comprehensively and with humility. The word "new" in our goal of a "new Ireland" had to be given unheard of and unquestionable hard substance. It would surprise, unsettle and shock those in the south, as well as those in the North, who believed either that this crisis would simply go away or that it could be solved by benign neglect or by violent conquest. This truly new beginning would have to confront the dilemma set out by Louis MacNeice, a great and fiercely honest Northern poet:

Why should I want to go back
To you, Ireland, my Ireland?
The blots on the page are so black
That they cannot be covered with shamrock.
I hate your grandiose airs,
Your sob-stuff, your laugh and your swagger,
Your assumption that everyone cares
Who is the king of your castle.
Castles are out of date,
The tide flows round the children's sandy fancy
Put up what flags you like, it is too late
To save your soul with bunting.

The Council for a New Ireland which the SDLP suggested and which when set up was called the Forum for a New Ireland would have to do more than confront these impossibilities: it would be called upon to reconcile and harmonise them and to forge a new, unheard-of, generous definition of Irishness which would include—not exclude—everything that was encompassed in being a Northern Protestant, including a sense of British identity. It would be called upon to cast this definition in the form of concrete proposals and concrete guarantees and to back up these proposals and guarantees with concrete action which would give unquestionable evidence of understanding, goodwill and resolute commitment.

The Taoiseach, Garret FitzGerald, had called the problem of Northern Ireland the greatest problem of Irish history. He was of course right. What I was proposing was a response to that problem which would call upon all the resources—intellectual, imaginative, economic, moral—of all Nationalist politicians in Ireland, in a united gesture of generosity to acknowledge and solve the crisis of our island, which was nothing less than the crisis of our own identity.

It was my view that this new body, committed to binding up the wounds of this country—having created an all-inclusive definition of Irishness and suggested forms of institutional expression, having proposed safeguards and roles for all our traditions—should then invite those whom they were intended to include, the Irish Protestant tradition, to tell us honestly how our proposals could be improved.

I saw this process as only the first of two major steps towards a solution. The first step, the harsh confrontation of the full dimensions of the issue and the definition in new and unheard-of terms of the new Ireland, would be followed by the presentation of a real and positive alternative, for the first time ever, to the men and women who had never so far considered such an eventuality.

I was under no illusions as to the problems or the difficulties that lay in the way, but if there was a political path to reconciliation of the major traditions of this island, it had to be charted, so that hope would replace the despair that paralysed our community. I was encouraged by the initial responses of the leaders in the Republic who had undertaken, together with their parties, to give our proposal the attention it deserved. We looked forward to early, detailed and fruitful discussions. To the followers of those Unionist leaders who had already predictably rejected our ideas we said, suspend judgment until you see the fruits of our deliberations. We would be happy to be judged then.

At that time—as the horizons darkened over our community, as the gunmen strutted our streets more brazenly, as our remaining economic muscle slackened to a final decline, as communal fear and despair mounted sickeningly with the rising toll of murder, as the intransigence of ignorance and bigotry hardened into roaring belligerency, as the British again retreated into their contemptuous indifference—it was plain that it was up to the patient men and women of the SDLP to gird ourselves to fight for the survival of life and reason in the North. For this we had to harden our wills and organise with all our determination.

We invited others to join us. It was no longer enough to leave it to the few. We had to expand our numbers and deepen our organisation in every quarter of Northern Ireland. We needed the help of all men and women of goodwill throughout Ireland. There was no time left for casual reflection—we were in a fight against time, anarchy, cruelty, stupidity and contempt. We could not, Northern Ireland could not, this island could not, allow ourselves to be distracted. There was a solution and we had to begin to construct it. We remained undaunted. It was too late to save our souls with bunting.

The SDLP did not allow itself to be distracted. In spite of the enormous problems of the 1980s, the SDLP grew in strength. In 1985, the Unionists resigned from Westminster as a protest against the Anglo-Irish Agreement, thereby causing by-elections. Seamus Mallon made a great breakthrough with his outstanding victory in Newry–Armagh, a victory which showed the widespread support we had for our overall strategy which had led to the Anglo-Irish Agreement. Seamus's victory also led to a great resurgence of energy in the party. In 1987, we gained another Westminster seat, with Eddie McGrady's historic victory over Enoch Powell. The SDLP went from strength to strength and Doctor Joe Hendron had another historic victory when he defeated Gerry Adams in the 1992 election, winning the crucial West Belfast seat. The detailed and selfless work of these elected colleagues powerfully strengthened the party and its message and became central to the evolution of the peace process. We have kept building and will continue to do so, relying as always on the dedicated and unflinching support and work of our grassroots membership.

— 9 —

The Hume–Adams Initiative

We hold the Ireland in the heart
More than the land our eyes have seen.
George Russell (AE)

If, in the aftermath of the 1994 ceasefires, this crucial time is not to become another of the "if onlys" of Irish history, it is imperative that we have immediate and profound reflection by all sections of our people, and in particular by all our political parties. Let none of us forget that the Provisional IRA and its members are a product of, among other things, the traditional Nationalist philosophy with which we in Ireland grew up, a philosophy that the essence of patriotism—*à la* 1916—was the noble act of dying for Ireland in the struggle against British occupation. All the major parties in the Dáil were born out of that philosophy and their founders were its progenitors.

If we are to achieve lasting peace on this island, the attitude and methods of Sinn Féin and the IRA will have to be addressed. In spite of the fact that they are a product of our history, the major responsibility rests with them to recognise that the philosophy of violence is obsolete and that there is no further justification for its continuance. The statistics of death, as I have outlined them in Chapter Seven, reveal that Republicans have killed six times more human beings than the British army, the RUC and the UDR together. In fact, more than half of the IRA deaths were perpetrated by their own members. The statistics also reveal that every year more than half of those killed were innocent civilians. Even if one believed in militarism, how could this be justified?

When I look back over the twenty-five years of the Troubles, I try not to single out any particular tragedy. My view remains that no bombing and no killing had any contribution to make in solving the problem. On the contrary, the violence worsened the situation. After IRA bombings in Britain, any subsequent chill from the politicians at Westminster only deepened the divisions and hardened Republican attitudes. It was a vicious and non-constructive cycle.

Furthermore, I could never see the tradition of hunger-strikes in Irish history—from Terence MacSwiney to Bobby Sands—as a vehicle for change. The H-Block hunger-strikes in 1981 led to ten people dying, creating enormous emotionalism across the country and recruiting a lot of young people into the IRA. While going on hunger-strike demonstrates the individual's own very strong commitment to their beliefs, it is still part of the psychology of violence of Irish patriotism which began early in this century. A hunger-strike is violence directed at the self.

I believe totally and absolutely in non-violence. I believe that every effort should always be made to achieve the peaceful resolution of all situations of conflict. Human beings should never be the instruments for ending human life, but, rather, the instruments for solving conflicts. The most fundamental human right of all is the right to life. How can we argue that we are fighting for human rights if our methods undermine the most fundamental human right of all?

When history is written, the Anglo-Irish Agreement will be seen to have been the first major step in the current peace process. In the Agreement, the British said that it would be incumbent upon those who wanted Irish unity to persuade those who did not. If the majority of people in Northern Ireland wanted Irish unity, they would have it. I pointed out that this declaration of British neutrality on the question of Irish unity removed the traditional justification for the use of force in Irish nationalism. However, Sinn Féin were quick to criticise me, demanding that I prove British neutrality. And so began a public debate between Sinn Féin and the SDLP.

That public debate led to the Northern Ireland Secretary Peter Brooke's speech of November 1990, in which he made it very clear that Britain no longer had any selfish interest in Northern Ireland, either economic or strategic.

In my first election campaign in 1969, my central point in challenging traditional nationalism was that it was the people of Ireland who were divided, not the territory, and that such division could only be healed by agreement. Our party—the SDLP—was the first party to put the word consent into its original constitution. That word is now central to the approach of all parties in the Dáil. Sinn Féin, in the very flexible language that they have used throughout the public debate on the peace process, have also moved in that direction. They have publicly agreed that any final solution must earn the allegiance of all our traditions.

Before this time I had only known Gerry Adams slightly. Our direct communication began with a letter I wrote to him on St. Patrick's Day in 1988, which led to the first public talks between our parties. When those talks failed, we issued a statement saying that we would continue the debate in public and in private. That private contact subsequently developed into the peace talks and the so-called Hume–Adams Initiative. The basic principles of that first letter remain central to our dialogue and the peace process to date.

When I first started talking to Adams, I found him to be totally straightforward in what he said to me, and we built a strong personal trust in one another, even though we had different opinions on many matters. It was this mutual regard and trust that was crucial to our success. Neither of us was playing party politics—we were both trying to solve a very grave problem.

The dialogue between Gerry Adams and myself concentrated on the two main traditional Republican reasons that provided the motivation for the IRA campaign. The first of these was that the British are in Ireland to defend their own economic and strategic interests by force. I argued that while that had certainly been true in the past—Ireland's historic links with Spain and France had provided a back door to Britain's European enemies, which Britain had wished to close—it was no longer true in today's new Europe, where Britain shares sovereignty not just with Ireland but with all her former European enemies down the centuries.

The other reason given by Sinn Féin was that the British were preventing the Irish people from exercising their right to self-determination. Gerry Adams and I agreed in our first joint statement of 1993 that, while the Irish people as a whole had the right to self-determination, they were divided as to how that right was to be exercised. The challenge was to harness all resources, particularly the British government's, in order to bring about such agreement. We decided that our dialogue would concentrate on the search for agreement and the means of reaching agreement. Since an agreement by coercion is a clear contradiction in terms, it was implicit that agreement had to be made freely and without the use of force.

My talks with Adams took place at a secret venue on a fairly regular basis over that period. In my opinion, had we maintained secrecy, we would have made progress much more quickly. However, our talks became public in 1993 and the resultant pressures and vilifications were awful, making life extremely difficult for both of us. Also, during that period, many of the homes of individual members of the SDLP were attacked, but my party maintained total solidarity with me and continued commitment to the talks between Adams and myself. There were enormous stresses and strains on all of us and, without the total solidarity of my colleagues, I could not have continued.

In explaining our talks, we issued a series of statements which made very clear our objectives—a total cessation of violence and the establishment of a dialogue process. Central to that process was the understanding that both governments and all parties with an electoral mandate—including Sinn Féin—would commit themselves to promoting agreement between all traditions, that it was for the Irish people alone, north and south, to decide what form the agreement would take, and that the British government would legislate accordingly.

Our talks would have failed without the full support of the Irish government. The then Taoiseach, Albert Reynolds, and Tánaiste Dick Spring began talks with the British government. The result was the Joint Declaration of December 1993, in which the British government declared that it no longer has any selfish, strategic or economic interests in Ireland, and that it is committed not only to promoting agreement between the divided people of Ireland, but also to legislating for any agreement that emerges from the representatives of the people. Clear self-determination!

The next challenge we face is to persuade the Unionists to sit around the table and embark on all-party talks. Until now they have always been able to rely on the British government to maintain their position, but what we are saying to them is that this problem cannot be solved without them, because of their geography and numbers. It is imperative that they grasp the nettle and seize this opportunity to protect their heritage.

People say a week is a long time in politics. However, a quarter of a century is a very short time in the history of a country, and I think that the fact that all parties now agree that all relationships have to be settled is great progress. The next stage is to get them all to sit around the same table.

In many ways what we need is a Unionist de Klerk. There are parallels between the South African situation and our own. If the solution to the problem in South Africa had been to draw a line on the map and create a small white state, with two whites to every black person, and to make the rest of South Africa independent, would there ever have been a possibility of peace? Would not the whites then have been forced to discriminate totally against the black minority in order to ensure that it never became a majority? This is precisely what happened in Ireland, and we are still living with the consequences.

I believe that we should follow the European example of evolution. Consider that, only fifty years ago, thirty-five million people lay dead across the continent of Europe. Nobody could have foreseen then that, fifty years later, there would be a united Europe. How did it happen? It happened because Europeans came to see that difference does not constitute a threat, that difference should in fact be respected, and that institutions should be built to work for our common interests. The process began with co-operation in the coal and steel industries and then developed into broader co-operation in solving economic and socio-economic problems. In this way, Europe has gradually broken down the barriers of centuries, and so evolved into a new Europe.

I hope that we can achieve something similar in Ireland, that we can create a framework which respects our differences, but allows us to work together in our common interests. Working together and producing results will build a trust that will help us to develop political agreement. From political agreement, we can build a better world for our children. The challenge facing us is not to find an instant package to solve the Irish problem but to create a framework that will facilitate a healing process, leading invariably and surely to a new Ireland.

— 10 —

Forum for Peace and Reconciliation

The old law of an eye for an eye leaves everybody blind.
Martin Luther King

When the British–Irish Joint Declaration was made in December 1993, I made clear that I regarded it as a major step on the road to peace, and I asked for it to be considered in detail by all parties before responding. Considering the importance of the declaration and its objective, that was not too much to ask. I also recognised that the most important response would be that of the Provisional Republican movement and that, given the nature of their organisation, that would take time. I also appealed for an absence of knee-jerk reaction. There was quite an amount of that, some of it irresponsible and inaccurate.

There was also a lot of unhelpful language like "take it or leave it", "decontamination periods" and "gauntlets", at a very sensitive and important time, particularly when the objective was to seek an end to all violence, to save human life and bring to an end the terrible tragedies that so many families have suffered. Language from some people who would describe themselves as Republicans was not helpful either, since their response was based on regarding the declaration as a settlement of our problems, which it is not. That will only come at the next stage of the process, involving both governments and all parties, hopefully in a totally peaceful atmosphere. What the Declaration essentially does, among other things, is to address again (as was done in 1985 and 1990) the stated reasons for armed struggle given by the IRA, as I outlined them in previous chapters.

In the Joint Declaration, the British Prime Minister, John Major, "reiterates on behalf of the British government that they have no selfish economic or strategic interest in Northern Ireland. Their primary interest"—which in my view is an acceptable and necessary political interest—"is to see peace, stability and reconciliation established by agreement among all the people who inhabit the island." He goes further and underlines that they would work together with the Irish government to achieve such an agreement, an agreement which would naturally have to address all the relationships that go to the heart of the problem.

I believe that the second stated reason of the IRA argument for armed struggle—self-determination—is clearly dealt with by the British government when they declare in the Joint Declaration: "The British government agree that it is for the people of the island of Ireland *alone*, by agreement between the two parts respectively, to exercise their right to *self-determination* on the basis of consent, *freely* and concurrently given, north and south, to bring about a united Ireland if that is their wish." To underline that commitment to self-determination by agreement among our divided people, they "reaffirm as a *binding* obligation that they will, for their part, introduce the necessary legislation to give effect to this [i.e. a united Ireland] or equally to any measure of agreement on future relationships in Ireland which the people living in Ireland may themselves *freely* so determine without external *impediment*."

Nothing could be clearer, and neither could the challenge to both traditions to bring about lasting stability and peace on our island by, for the first time, reaching such agreement. It is surely self-evident that anyone who genuinely wants such agreement would recognise that it can never be achieved by any form of coercion or force. The task is for everyone involved to commit all their energies to working for such agreement. There has been the usual talk of vetoes. Again, it is clear that, when you have a divided people, each section of it has a veto, but that is a negative way of looking at it—and we have never had any shortage of negative attitudes on this island. Surely the time has come to be positive, and to seek and work for agreement, the challenge of which is to persuade one another that neither side wants victory, but each wants an agreement which respects our different heritages and identities, which is the only basis for stability in any society.

In addition, the British government, while not using the word persuade, commit themselves to "*encourage*, facilitate and enable the achievement of such agreement over a period through a process of dialogue and co-operation based on full respect for the rights and identities of both traditions in Ireland". If we do not want them to impose a solution, which is not self-determination, what more can they do? When, at any time in the past seventy years, have both governments been so committed to using all their influence, energy and resources towards such an objective?

None of this is to suggest that the problem has been solved, but it does underline that, while past reasons given by the Republican movement for armed struggle no longer apply, the legacy of that past which remains and which is today's problem cannot be resolved by force. It also confirms the need for the second main request of Sinn Féin, put repeatedly in statements and speeches to the Irish government and the SDLP, for an organised political alternative to tackle the problem. That alternative had been clearly offered by the then Taoiseach, Albert Reynolds, in establishing a Forum for Peace and Reconciliation, to face up to the challenges that face us if we are to resolve peacefully the problems of our divided people in a manner that threatens no section of our island race. The creation of such a forum was a central proposal of the SDLP in its 1988 talks with Sinn Féin, and remained central in my talks with Gerry Adams.

The challenge that now faces all of us is a clear *political* challenge—how to heal the deep divisions among the people of Ireland, divisions which have social and, above all, economic implications, particularly for the areas of high unemployment within the North and the border counties. In meeting this challenge we will be working together, not only to harness the positive energies and talents of all our people, but to harness as well the powerful international goodwill that arises from the fact that we are the biggest wandering people in the world.

If all Northern parties come together with the south, for the first time since 1920, that representation will ensure that all problems will be consistently and positively addressed. It will have a powerful social and economic impact, which is what all politics should be about. Wrapping the flag around our young people and pride in our Irishness are not of much value if those young people have to earn their living in another land or spend their lives in dole queues in our own.

There is free movement of goods, people and services throughout Ireland in the new Europe without land borders. The British army checkpoints were the only remaining signs of a border anywhere in the new Europe, and they are now disappearing with peace. Natural social and economic activity has resumed for the first time in seventy years, particularly in the border regions. Indeed, research carried out by business leaders has already indicated that the development to the full of the economic potential of internal free trading with Ireland as a whole will create 75,000 jobs.

I have not mentioned, of course, the special assistance that will come from our friends throughout Europe as well—as has already been indicated by present European leaders. Let us not forget that our problems with Britain were European in origin. Ireland historically has always had positive links with Europe—links which were interrupted to

Irish disadvantage by the English presence in Ireland. We are now totally free—particularly if we are organised—to resume and develop our links across Europe for the benefit of all our people and giving hope in particular to our young people.

The other deep problem that we face, a problem that will be eroded by economic development, is the division in the hearts and minds of our people. Partition is not the Irish problem. It simply institutionalised and exacerbated the differences that had been there for centuries. Those differences go back even beyond the Plantation of Ulster, because of our geography and our special geographical relationship with the neighbouring island. In the sixth century, St. Columba returned from Iona and, at the Convention of Drumceat, settled a bitter and bloody quarrel between the clans in Antrim, the Dál Riada—who claimed their loyalty to the King of Argyll—and the clans in Tyrone, Derry and Donegal, whose loyalties were to Irish kings. His solution was to let them pay tribute to both!

Indeed, is it not a deep misunderstanding of the Ulster Protestant tradition that it is only British influence and not their own deeply-felt reasons that up until now have made them want to live apart from the rest of the people of Ireland, reasons that go back beyond partition, as indeed the founder of Irish republicanism, Wolfe Tone, underlined when he spoke of the need to unite Catholic, Protestant and Dissenter, implicitly admitting that they were divided. Although some of them might find it offensive to speak of their siege mentality, there is no doubt that this dominates their political mentality. Although today they are not colonists nor settlers, like the rest of us their heritage and attitudes come down from a past for which they are not responsible. There is a strong settler element in the deep-seated fear of revenge which underlies the siege mentality.

This underlines the necessity to recognise that the Unionist people are just as much victims of the past as we are, and strengthens the challenge to all of us to show that we mean what we say when we talk of an Ireland that will respect the democratic dignity and civil rights of both communities.

The challenge that we now face is to remove the last remaining legacy of imperialism in Europe—the deep divisions among our island people—and to do so in a manner that respects our basic humanity and our diversity. It is an enormous challenge to all of us. It is a challenge that requires from the Republican movement one of the greatest acts of moral courage of this century. But, in the final analysis, it is moral courage that endows real leadership and creates truly historic opportunity.

If we contrast the gloomy prospect of twenty-five years of armed struggle to the vision of twenty-five years of committed peaceful and organised activity, harnessing all the energies of our people to face up to our problems and to promote and develop consistently the healing process, should there be any doubt about our choice for the next generation?

As we face the twenty-first century, the time has come to leave the past behind us. Most of our politics has been about the wrongs committed by the other side, but we must now be prepared to look to the future. We must ensure that the next century is the first in our island history that is not scarred by the gun and the bomb, and create, at last, an island whose institutions have the allegiance of all our traditions and respect our diversity. Together we can use all our energies to build a new Ireland in the new Europe of which we are already a part. Let us commit ourselves to spilling our sweat and not our blood.

What is very necessary at this crucial time in our history is that there is clear confidence in all sections of our community. That is why in every statement issued by Gerry Adams and myself we have made clear that our ultimate objective is agreement among our divided people on this island, an agreement that must earn the allegiance of all traditions. That, to me, is common sense because victories are not solutions in divided societies. In many ways Northern

Ireland politics has always been about the past, but the time has come to draw a line under that past and let history judge it, and let us look to a future for the first time in which we can reach an agreement that respects our diversity. Our eyes must be on the horizon.

A united Europe is the greatest example of conflict resolution in the history of the world, given the centuries of previous conflict, and it is the duty of everyone to study how this was achieved. Put simplistically, conflict occurs when people see difference as a threat. Difference is the essence of humanity. There are not two human beings in the world who are the same, and difference, whether of colour, nationality or creed, should never be the source of hatred or conflict. The peoples of Europe learned to create institutions which respected their diversity but allowed them to profit from their common ground—economics. Thus the healing process began and the prejudice of centuries has been gradually eroded. Peace came slowly dropping.

I believe that we must do the same in Ireland. We must create, by agreement, institutions which respect our diversity but allow us to work together. If this happens a new Ireland will evolve, very different from the traditional models of the past, but based on agreement, earning the allegiance of all our traditions.

I believe that the Forum for Peace and Reconciliation, suggested by the then Taoiseach, Albert Reynolds, in the Downing Street Declaration, and subsequently created by his government, should have a major role to play in this process. It is the view of the SDLP that one of its major tasks would be to plan how we can break down the barriers of prejudice and distrust that divide our people, and to take practical steps to do so. I have no doubt that this will take time, but if it takes place in an entirely peaceful atmosphere it will be easier to make progress.

Its other objective should be, in conjunction with the Irish abroad, particularly in the United States, to re-build our country economically, concentrating on areas of high unemployment in the North. The positive results of the peace process will then be visible to our young people, who will be able to earn a living in the land of their birth. I am aware from my contacts with the American political and business community, where people of Irish extraction are prominent in both, that they are very keen to help us. They are already doing so through the International Fund for Ireland, which has created 27,000 jobs. As the European experience has shown, reconstruction goes hand in hand with reconciliation. It is the other side of the coin.

I have of course suggested on a number of occasions that I would like the Unionist people also to create a Forum in which they too would address the question of how to protect their heritage and break down the barriers of prejudice and distrust that divide us, so that we can eventually reach agreement. Naturally they, too, could develop links with their own powerful tradition in Canada and the United States to tackle our significant economic problems. If both Forums worked together on that non-controversial front, it could be a major part of the process of building trust.

I would also like both Forums to commit themselves, in the old Presbyterian tradition, to a Covenant of Honour which would protect the heritage of both our traditions in Ireland and release our considerable energies and talents to build a new island of which we could all be proud. Let us now face our primary challenge, which is to create the institutions that will achieve just that.

There has been a lot of public discussion and a lot of careless language by politicians, both British and Irish, in relation to our future, or their preferences about that future. However, at this crucial point of time it is essential that we concentrate on the facts of our situation in Ireland and the facts of the Joint Declaration—the most comprehensive statement by British and Irish governments in seventy years on our relationships within this island.

Let us stay with the facts. The people of Ireland have the right to determine their own future, but what gets consistently forgotten as people make emotional declarations about such rights, is that it is people who have rights. The essence of settling differences is to respect them and there is not a single stable society in the world that is not based on respect for difference.

The people of Ireland are divided as to how to exercise their right to self-determination, so are the people in the former Yugoslavia, so are the people of the world. It is the search for agreement and the means of reaching agreement that is the real task at hand. It is also surely a fact that such agreement among divided peoples anywhere cannot be solved by any form of coercion or force. Victories, as history has sadly taught us, are not solutions—they simply leave a legacy from which subsequent generations also suffer.

Through the Joint Declaration, the British government have made clear, not for the first time, that, whatever about the past, they no longer have any selfish or strategic interests in Ireland.

The challenge to all is clear. To the Unionist tradition, who have a genuinely different heritage from the rest of us in this island, and who have every right to protect that heritage, the challenge is to recognise for the first time that their real strength rests in their own numbers and their own geography, and the problem cannot be solved without them. Have they the self-confidence to stand on their own feet, recognising that the only people that they need to trust in such a process are themselves? It is self-evident that they have consistently distrusted British governments. Now they are being asked to trust themselves and to recognise that the objective is an agreement which must earn the allegiance of all our traditions, including their own.

The challenge to the Nationalist tradition is equally clear, particularly the challenge to Sinn Féin and the IRA. Have they the confidence in their own convictions to come to the table armed only with those convictions and their powers of persuasion, as everyone else will have to do, given that the British government is now committed not only to encouraging agreement but to implementing and legislating for whatever agreement emerges?

We have reached a historic moment in our island's history and my hope is that the moral courage will be there on all sides to seize it. It is to me self-evident that no instant package will end our differences forever; but whatever form our agreement takes, once our quarrel is over and all the talents of our diverse people are committed to working together to build our country, north and south, the healing process will have begun and the old prejudices and distrusts will be progressively eroded. Europe is the model as to how quickly old animosities can fade. Down the road, out of that process will emerge a new Ireland, built on respect for our diversity, whose model will probably be very different from any of our past traditional models. Will Catholic, Protestant and Dissenter finally come together in our small island and, as we approach the twenty-first century of a post-Nationalist and interdependent world, will we at last remove the gun and the bomb from our politics and our people?

Part Five

A New Ireland

— 11 —

Peace Be Within Thy Walls

A dreamer lives forever
And a toiler dies in a day.
John Boyle O'Reilly

Following the announcement on 31 August 1994 of a cessation of military activities by the Irish Republican Army, closely followed by a similar declaration by the Loyalist paramilitaries, we enjoyed a new era of peace in Ireland. Sinn Féin, the political wing of the IRA, committed itself to peaceful and democratic means to reach an agreement between the people of Ireland that can earn the allegiance of all our traditions, and we must do everything to ensure that the dialogue leading to such agreement takes place in a totally peaceful atmosphere.

That was the clearly stated objective of my dialogue with Gerry Adams. Since five British governments and twenty thousand troops had failed to stop the violence, I took the view that, if the killing of human beings on our streets could be ended by direct dialogue, then it was my duty to attempt to do just that. I am naturally pleased that we were able to achieve this first step towards lasting stability.

Now we must move on to our next major challenge: to reach agreement between two fundamentally different mind-sets—the Unionist and the Nationalist.

In my approach to the process of reconciliation, I have

been strongly inspired by both my European experience and my contact with the United States. The European Union is a great testament to the resolution of conflict. Today, Europeans are engaged in a level of co-operation so intense that it has blurred the traditional bounds of sovereignty and notions of territorial integrity. Similarly, the political system of the United States commands the loyalty of citizens despite the diversity of their ethnic make-up and experience. Each American citizen carries in the small change in his or her pocket the maxim that unites the country: *e pluribus unum*, from many we are one. It cannot be said too often; it works.

We in Ireland are now engaged in a process that seeks to give reality to this powerful aspiration. We must create, by agreement, as was done in post-war Europe, institutions that respect our diversity but allow us also to work our substantial economic ground together. Through this process, it will be possible for a new Ireland to evolve. My confident hope is that the fast-approaching twenty-first century will be the first in our island's history in which the evil genius of mistrust and violence will finally be laid to rest. The ghosts of our nation, to paraphrase Pearse, may have been appeased enough. It is now time for the living.

While we work for political agreement, we should also work together to build our country economically, so that the positive results of the peace process can be visible to our young people.

Any agreement emerging from talks involving both governments and all parties must recognise and recruit the legitimacy of each tradition—Unionist and Nationalist. We cannot embrace or express the equal validity of both traditions if we do not allow for dual validation of a new, agreed political dispensation. The SDLP's proposal for a dual referendum would meet this requirement in a way that diminishes no tradition nor any assurances it has or needs.

It is essential to tackle the problem on a holistic rather than a reductionist level. We must assess problems within their wider context and develop new relationships and structures. This has very important lessons for Ireland and Britain, not just with regard to advancing relationships between both islands, but also to pursuing those relationships within the context of the changing European order.

This change in the European order is continuing apace at two levels. One is the growing integration of the European Union based on the realisation that the democratic nation state is no longer a sufficient political entity to allow people to have adequate control over the economic and technological forces which affect people's opportunities and circumstances. (The task is to ensure that those arrangements and institutions which develop shared policies and programmes are democratically based. The issue is the need to optimise the real sovereignty of the peoples of Europe rather than ossifying our democratic development around limited notions of national sovereignty which only give space to multi-national vested interest.)

The other level at which the European order is changing is with respect to the transforming scene in Eastern and Central Europe, which has opened the prospect of the Common European Home.

The strengthening of the European Union offers a framework for international relations which is accepted as an essential and effective way in which the whole breadth of Europe can enjoy greater security with each other. We can only obtain real security in alliance with others, rather than in defence against them. This has significance in British and Irish relationships, because it underscores the fact that, whatever strategic considerations inspired British attitudes to Ireland in the past, these are now obsolescent, if not already obsolete.

However, the European Union dimension has significance beyond the strategic consideration. It represents a changing economic interface between countries. The process of the Single European Market demonstrates unarguably that whatever economic considerations historically informed British policy on Ireland, these can no longer be held to apply.

Ongoing economic integration in the European Union is diminishing the relevance of notions that Britain does, or can, defend a singular economic self-interest by its presence, and financial outlay, in Northern Ireland. Furthermore, the nature of the EU's development belies any suggestion that Britain's position in Ireland today is guided by strategic interests. I repeat again that Britain has stated categorically and consistently, since the 1985 Anglo-Irish Agreement, that it has no selfish strategic or economic interest in Northern Ireland.

It is true that, historically, British involvement in Ireland was motivated by strategic sensitivities and economic selfishness, but the situation is now very different. Britain is pooling sovereignty, not just with France and Spain, but with Ireland and other European countries as well. This is fundamentally changing British–Irish relations. The two governments now participate in the ongoing process of addressing the ever-expanding range of EU issues. Common membership of a new Europe moving towards unity, has provided a constructive context for the discussion and exercise of sovereignty in these islands.

This is a context where there is increasing acceptance that policies and agencies operating only on a nation state basis cannot properly cope with wider economic and technological forces, or trends which bear on our social circumstances and impact on our environment.

If democracy is to keep pace with reality, we have to operate programmes which can better match the scale and scope of those factors which require democratic control, if the needs and will of the people are to prevail. Shared sovereignty and interdependence are, therefore, of supreme importance, because this is the method by which we can maximise democratic policy-making.

The traditional notions of absolute and indivisible national sovereignty and territorial jealousy are now so inadequate that their promotion is destructive. It is important that the debate on European harmonisation is based on the right questions—not least in Britain. The emphasis must be, not on whether national sovereignty is being diluted, but whether democracy is being dilated.

All this clearly has significance for Ireland, given that the historic difficulties in relationships within the island, and between Britain and Ireland, have hinged on attitudes and aspirations concerning sovereignty, territory, and the achievement or maintenance of separateness. The new European scene offers a psychological framework in which such issues can no longer be pursued in absolutist terms. There is growing appreciation that interdependence can be achieved without sacrificing independence. The importance of this for a situation which has been described as one of "conflicting nationalisms" should not be overlooked.

Some Irish Nationalists, and also some Unionists, have indicated that they regard European integration as the enemy's "latest trick". For one side, the European Union is suspect because it undermines national sovereignty, and because the British have particular influence. For the other, it undermines UK sovereignty and is a device which will remove the border in Ireland by stealth.

In perceiving the EU as an alien arrangement, contriving threats to their identity, they, like the europhobes in Britain, are confirming an inherent lack of self-confidence in the very identity and values which, they claim, distinguish their people. However, it is to be hoped that experience of the European process will have an educative effect on such attitudes. Issues will be seen in a wider context than the narrow ground of our traditionally disputed local political arena. Other nations with profound historical and cultural differences can be seen to be working together, compromising and co-operating, through agreed institutions and frameworks, without any sacrifice of principle.

The EU's structures were designed to allow diverse peoples to grow together at their own speed. They also allow the EU institutions themselves to change and develop, in their purpose and operation, to keep pace with that growth, and with social, economic and environmental realities. There are lessons here for us, in our quest for political frameworks to accommodate diverse interests and identities, promote co-operation, provide for common needs, and allow for agreed development and adjustment in the future.

I believe that we are benefiting from exposure to a political ethos and modalities which are not as psychologically constraining as the ethos of "winner takes all" and the constitutional stagnancy of the British system. Both Unionists and Nationalists have always sought to express their rights in terms of their territorial majority, and other norms of the British system and nineteenth-century nationalism, but it is becoming ever more apparent that there are other valid norms which we can assimilate.

The changes that have taken place in Europe offer us the challenge and inspiration to seek to replace bitter conflict and tension with co-operation and partnership, without anyone being cast as victor or vanquished, and without loss of anyone's distinctiveness or identity.

In this regard, it is surely instructive to observe how France and Germany needed to find a wider forum to bring about lasting reconciliation. The sheer intensity and massiveness of the historical pressure towards division were transformed in the broader context of the original European Community.

It is also significant that the Community came into being in limited areas which were at the heart of the relationships between the founding countries. They began with their common ground. They began, in fact, with the coal and steel industries, and sovereignty was pooled in these areas.

If countries and peoples that slaughtered one another in their millions, twice in this century alone, can lay aside their past, can build institutions which respect their differences, allowing them to work their common ground together, we can draw great hope from that simple, but profound event.

Further, given that both parts of Ireland have already voted for that European process, have agreed to the pooling of sovereignty and new relations with Greeks, French, Germans, Spanish, Dutch, Danes, and others, is it not long past the time when we should build new relationships with one another?

The Single Europe and the whole ongoing process of integration will continue to have an important impact on the border, as we know it, in Ireland. This should neither be exaggerated nor underestimated. The process will allow the border to ebb substantially from economic life on the island, and will provide a context which will require, and should inspire, policy programmes and administrative instruments which will be cross-border and all-Ireland in scope. Such a scenario was very well outlined in a British Labour Party policy document on Ireland.

This in itself cannot remove the political division. Yet it will allow the real essence of that division to be addressed, rather than being distorted and exacerbated by economic, social and administrative divergences and rivalries.

It is not Panglossian to suggest that people from both traditions in Ireland can absorb the lessons of European harmonisation and achieve convergence in the expression and pursuit of their identities and interests. A European dimension is hardly a new factor in Ireland's long-running problems. Remember that events celebrated by Unionists, such as the Siege of Derry in 1689 and the Battle of the Boyne in 1690, were not just local religious battles. They were part of a much wider European power game. On the Republican and Nationalist side, Wolfe Tone is generally regarded as the "father" of Irish republicanism. His inspiration came from the French Revolution and its intellectual protagonists, while French military assistance was central to his strategy for rebellion.

Hence both traditions—Unionist invoking of "civil and religious liberty", or Nationalist espousal of Republican ideals—have derived much of their strength or rationale from events or ideals originating elsewhere in the Europe of the past. Is it too much to suggest that we can share in the spirit of the changing Europe of the present and future?

Having demonstrated the potential for new relationships within Ireland, and between Ireland and Britain, against the background of a changing Europe, I should perhaps also indicate something of the role which I perceive that Ireland might play in that context.

Ireland has remained neutral from military alliances, whatever its democratic or ideological affinities, and current developments serve more to vindicate that position than invalidate it. They also, however, call for a realignment of that neutrality to update it to present realities and potential achievements.

I am not suggesting that Ireland join NATO, whose relevance is more questionable now than previously, with the collapse of the Soviet Empire, but that Ireland could identify a common cause, not just with other neutral Western states, but also with countries of Central and Eastern Europe who want to escape, responsibly, from the notion of two military conglomerates. In doing so, Ireland could play a role that would complement the efforts of those member states in NATO who want to work to achieve real and complete pan-European security, offering true peace rather than maintaining intra-European defensive modes, albeit with less tension.

I think that Ireland has a particularly strong interest in ensuring that European policies and programmes carry a strong regional orientation, in order to safeguard the democratic effectiveness and legitimacy of the Single Europe and the equity of its policies. I suspect that, in this, we would have common cause with people in the various regions of Britain and in many other countries besides.

Furthermore, I believe that an Ireland at peace with itself, and at peace with its neighbour, can properly address itself, in its European activities, to what is almost a political calling to maintain a particular regard for the rights and needs of the developing world. As the only state in the European Union to have been colonised rather than to have colonised, we should be able to promote an intelligent empathy with the under-developed countries whose peoples can benefit most effectively from European Union policies. As a country that has suffered famine and under-development, we know that these hardships and obscenities are not simply the product of natural disasters but rather result from exploitation, unequal power relationships, unjust economic relationships, and an indifference to our common humanity. This should inspire us to persuade and support others in the pursuit of a new international economic order. Ireland, all of it, has a pivotal role to play.

These considerations combine to suggest that the new Ireland would not be at a point of arrival, but rather at a point of departure, on a challenging and progressive journey, where it could maturely discharge a responsibility to, and with, the other peoples with whom it shares this continent. It should find its peace in a new Europe and, in so doing, find its place in working for a better world.

— 12 —

The Future of Ireland

Each age is a dream that is dying
Or one that is coming to birth.
Arthur O'Shaughnessy

The completion of the European internal market will effect great change in Ireland, change in relations within the island of Ireland and change in relations between this island and the outside world.

Its completion is only one dimension of a transformation which is now inexorably and irreversibly under way in the European Union and which is leading towards the creation of a single political and economic entity. However sceptical the British may be, political union in Europe is firmly on the agenda, and the European partners are deadly serious about it. All of the various elements which go to make up a single political and economic entity are being moved into place. Absolutely free movement of goods, services and labour are the ingredients of a single market. But discussion is also taking place in relation to harmonising standards, taxation systems (including personal taxation), social security systems, the creation of a single currency and the creation of a Union-wide code of common rights. Such rights will encompass standards of health care, educational provision, and rights of workers in the workplace. It will mean that a code of rights in every sphere of life will be the entitlement of every citizen of the European Union. Economic and social integration on this scale must lead to the development of integrated political institutions in order to realise democratic control.

I say all of this in order to establish the complete context in which we have to look at our future on this island. I say "our future" deliberately, because we are going to face the same future and we have no option but to face it together, and on the same terms. We will, however, shape it more successfully to our advantage if we co-operate in exploiting our common strengths and addressing our common weaknesses.

Thankfully, people in the business world are largely unencumbered by history or the baggage of past tribal conflicts. Instances of co-operation and amalgamation in business and industry, between the two parts of this island, are multiplying in number and in scale. One only has to look at the food sector to see the truth of this—at the number of meat plants in the North that are in southern hands and the moves that are going on in the dairy co-operatives. Also, the timber processing plants in the North are extending their interests all over the country. And the commodity that is so dear to many Irish hearts—whiskey, literally in Irish the "water of life"—which is produced in a variety of forms in both parts of the island, is now jointly marketed throughout the world.

We are rapidly becoming one economy. This trend will accelerate as Europe integrates, because it makes sense for businesses in both parts of the island to gear themselves on an all-Ireland scale, in order to face the challenge of competition in the single market.

My city, Derry, represents a microcosm of the Irish situation and how it can work in the future. The city council, which was known as Derry Corporation, had control of housing and planning; it was abolished and an independent commission was set up to run the city until such time as the voting system was changed and proportional representation was introduced. In 1973, the first democratic council was elected in the city and the SDLP became the major party.

Since then, rather than in any way to appear to seek revenge, and in fact to make clear that revenge is not part of our philosophy, our approach has been, at all times, to show respect for each of our different traditions. This is evident in the way we govern the city. We alternate the mayor each year: one year SDLP, next year Unionist. The chairs of committees in the city council go to different parties; the SDLP could have taken all seats, all chairs, but we did not. While not removing the political differences, what such equality does is create a team spirit. We have created an institution—the city council—which respects difference, but works the common ground together, and the common ground is the city.

The team spirit is reflected in the fact that the atmosphere in Derry, as most objective observers would note, has changed substantially and there is now an amount of cross-community activity in the city. In recent times, following meetings with Mayor Ray Flynn, I have set up a cross-community body to attract inward investment and market the products of our small companies. It started out as Derry–Boston Ventures, and now it is known as Northwest International. The board of the body is drawn from both sections of the community and they work very solidly together. They have taken companies from all over Northern Ireland to America, to market their products, and there have been forty-two million dollars worth of orders to date. This has attracted major investment into the city.

One of the advantages we have in dealing with the outside world is the enormous fund of goodwill that exists for Ireland and the Irish all over the world. That goodwill is a major advantage in doing business abroad. It is also an important source of strength in our search for inward investment, which is so badly needed if we are to tap the full potential of this country and create work for all its people. A prime example of what can be done is the McCarter Fruit of the Loom initiative in the north-west, which has huge potential in both jurisdictions. The yarn is spun in Derry, while knitting, dyeing and making up are completed in Donegal for the European and world markets.

The Boston Development Grouping, O'Connell Brothers, initiated the development of the Foyle riverside of Derry. When this was completed it created, together with the government development beside it, 1,200 jobs. It will double the number of people who come into the city to shop. Seagate has chosen Derry as its European base, again through our contacts in America. It is Silicon Valley's endorsement of our efforts. It employs 850 people. Such investments help to tackle the serious unemployment problem which still plagues the city. I believe that we have demonstrated very clearly that our philosophy in practice could be an example to other areas of Northern Ireland.

It was not just goodwill which generated such investments. We have solid advantages to offer investors. We are the first stop on the way from America to Europe, and we offer the most convenient entry point into the European market, which is now the biggest in the world. We speak the same language as Americans, have an extensive common cultural heritage, and the same broad social and political values. We have a relatively clean environment, a beautiful and uncluttered country and an educated workforce.

My position as a public representative means that I meet directly with various contacts and seek their assistance in approaching companies that are looking for locations in Europe. My big argument to them is that we are not looking for charity, but that we are offering them a foothold in the biggest single market in the world, the European Single Market. We can give the highest level of public assistance to a company setting up in our region, as we get special European assistance to attract investors.

We have also worked hard to develop the infrastructure of our city. Given that we are right on the periphery of north-west Europe, transportation is hugely important. With help from the European Commission, we have been able to build a new harbour, which we have moved to deeper water, away from the city centre. This allows much bigger ships to come in, and it has also cleared some of the dead land in the city centre for urban renewal. Our new airport, funded by Europe and the European Commission, allows access to virtually anywhere in the world.

None of that would have been possible without the regeneration programme, assisted by our membership of the European Union. There is no doubt that membership has been of major benefit to our region. Not only has it funded infrastructure in transport—airports, harbours and roads—but it has also enabled us to give maximum public assistance to industries that locate in our area—up to fifty per cent of start-up costs, plus funding for training programmes for young people to suit incoming industries.

There is a great spirit of self-help in Derry. We believe that there is no point in simply complaining and doing nothing. Our heads and hands are as good as anybody else's, so we are using them to develop our own city. Politically and socially, people are working together. The church leaders in our city have given good example by working closely together. We now have a joint cathedral annual musical festival in the city—no one would have foreseen that, even ten years ago. We try to demonstrate that difference is natural. People are born into different cultures, societies, religions, and our challenge is to respect difference and to work together.

We still have a long way to go, particularly in the area of unemployment, and, hopefully, we will be able to keep our young people at home. However, a lot of groups have been set up in Derry. The Inner City Trust, led by Paddy Doherty, which involves groupings across the community, has rebuilt the entire inner city, employing young people, training them and other community groups to build in the city. Community centres and shopping centres are being built by the people, for the people. As a result of all these factors, the level of violence has dropped. Derry was the place where the Troubles started in the early seventies. The violence in Derry was worse than anywhere else. A lot of the city was burned and there was terrible street violence. But, in the late eighties, the violence dropped considerably. One of the reasons for that was the team spirit that was developing in the city, the way people were working together to rebuild it.

The violence in the North, and the continuing political uncertainty there, has created a negative image which affects the whole country. Solving that problem is the absolute priority of my party, because, until it is solved, we have a ball and chain around our ankles.

In fact, the economic problems and disadvantages that we are facing are common to both parts of Ireland: scarcity of jobs, resulting in unemployment and the emigration of many of the best of our young people, distance from markets for our produce, the under-employment of small and medium-size farmers throughout the disadvantaged areas of the country, and deep-rooted poverty in a large section of the population. If we are to solve these problems, I believe we need to develop long-term strategies, and there is a compelling argument for a joint approach. We can achieve most by pooling our efforts, north and south, in a more comprehensive way than we have managed to do so far.

The essence of unity and stability in any society is the acceptance of diversity. Paradoxically, the exclusivism which unionism appears to us to represent in our society is in total contradiction of those values that Protestantism represents in world culture: freedom of conscience, liberty of the individual, civil and religious freedoms.

I have spoken of the role of the Ulster Protestant in the creation of the United States of America and its Constitution. There they helped to create a society in which the enormous differences are respected and they all work together in the common interest—the real task of politics—to improve people's way of life. This philosophy, as I have noted before, can be summed up in the epitaph on the grave of Abraham

Lincoln, *e pluribus unum*. Nothing could contrast more to the continuing message of Protestant Unionists.

The Nationalist people, largely from the Catholic community, must also re-examine their attitudes. Many of our young people became involved in physical force movements—or armed struggle, as they called it—in keeping with a handed-down notion of Irish patriotism. Those who claimed the right to kill and the right to die in the name of Irish unity not only contradict the meaning of unity, but undermine the integrity of the concept. Their philosophy is clearly not about unity of people, but about conquest, assimilation or triumphalism. To make the most fundamental human right—the right to live—subsidiary to a political principle—the right to self-determination—is to undermine all human rights.

Self-determination is the language of the League of Nations and of the United Nations, but it derives from a period in world history when the nation state was the essential concept of government and is based on territorial interests. Territory was more important than people. That is the basic philosophy which fuelled nineteenth- and early twentieth-century nationalism and led to imperialism and two world wars.

Thankfully, the rest of Western Europe—but unfortunately not Eastern Europe—has moved away from that concept. The world is a much smaller place today, not least because of development in telecommunications and transport. Interdependence has become more important than independence. We cannot live in isolation.

I must reiterate how important it is that we recognise that it is people who have rights, not an abstract piece of land. When a people are divided as to how these rights are to be exercised, then agreement cannot be achieved by any form of force or coercion. In fact, as we know from sad and bitter experience, coercion in any form, particularly violence, only drives people further apart and deepens their divisions. We are human beings before we are anything else. Humanity transcends nationality or identity. That is not only a fundamentally Christian statement, it is the basis of lasting peace anywhere in the world.

What we must achieve, if we are to have lasting peace, is agreement on how we live together on the island of Ireland. The terrible price of our disagreement does not have to be spelt out. We lived with it daily in human, social and economic terms, and it is an insult to the common Christianity of our island.

In order to underline our commitment to agreement, the SDLP have proposed—and this has been endorsed by the Irish government—that any agreement reached should be endorsed in a joint referendum, held on the same day in the North and in the Republic and requiring a "Yes" from each.

This proposal is designed to reassure the Unionist people that we mean what we say when we talk of agreement. From a Unionist perspective, such an agreement would not just be validated by a majority of people in the North, but would have the approval and allegiance of Nationalist Ireland—north and south.

From a Nationalist point of view, it would be the first time ever that the people of Ireland as a whole would have endorsed the institutions of government, north and south. This is the true basis of lasting peace and order, because, for the first time ever, the institutions of government would have the total loyalty of all the people.

The British government has made clear that it not only wants to see agreement between the people of Ireland as to how they will live together, but that it will do all in its power to facilitate such agreement and, if agreement is reached, that it will respect such an agreement. It goes without saying that any such agreement would have to concentrate on giving positive expression to relationships within Ireland, as well as to the unique relationships which exist between Britain and Ireland.

Such agreement should be much easier today than fifty years ago. We live together in a Europe which has sorted out much deeper differences and we have a duty to learn from the European experience. European peoples slaughtered one another twice in this century alone. Yet, today, we have a unity which respects the widespread diversity and dignity of the peoples of Western Europe, setting aside bitterness and distrust. It is our duty to examine how it was done and apply the lessons to areas of conflict everywhere.

The people of Western Europe have accepted that difference is not a threat. They have learned to respect it and to build institutions which accommodate it and allow the people to work their common ground together, the common ground being the economy. That is precisely the approach that we should adopt and that is the approach that has governed our attitudes and proposals so far in the peace process.

In keeping with that approach, we defined our problem as the need to accommodate two sets of legitimate rights—the rights of the Unionist people to their identity, their ethos and their way of life, and the right of the Nationalist people to precisely the same. We believe that, in the context of the new Europe, in which sovereignty has changed its meaning and whose very existence is a proclamation that the independent nation state is out of date, it should be easier for us to resolve our differences.

Our situation today is totally different from the 1920s, where our problem was a straightforward clash of sovereignties. Today, both British and Irish governments are sharing sovereignty over our most fundamental interests with many other countries and are committed, by international agreement, to "an ever closer European Union".

If we take the positive view, Nationalists can take comfort from the fact that an ever closer union applies to both parts of Ireland within Europe, while Unionists can draw comfort from the fact that an ever closer union exists between Britain and Ireland in the new Europe. It remains for us to sort out our own relationships, so that we can take responsibility for the matters that affect all our people and create the circumstances in which we will at last work together in our common interests.

That was the thinking that governed our proposals to the talks before the ceasefire, the accommodation of both identities. We proposed that three commissioners be elected by proportional representation and that they would, as in the American presidential tradition, each appoint two experts from the community as a whole to administer the six departments of government in Northern Ireland. These elected commissioners would be joined by nominees from Dublin and London. In our view, these proposals give strong recognition to the Unionist identity and minimal recognition to our own. The Unionists would have six members in the administration, we would have three. In addition, Northern Ireland would still be in the United Kingdom, with representation at Westminster. The only expression of Nationalist identity would be the nominee from Dublin, who would be matched on the Unionist side by one from London.

We also suggested that the administration should, like the European Council of Ministers, act unanimously for a number of years, thus ensuring that we would work together on common ground. This would build trust and confidence and would rule out any threat of take-over. In our view, Unionist objections to our proposals, and their misrepresentation of them, were not really objections to the actual proposals, but were an expression of their distrust that there might be ulterior intentions or a hidden agenda. They were ignoring our total commitment to agreement, as expressed in our joint referendum proposals. Perhaps they were back with the negative and exclusive mind-set that believes there is only one set of legitimate rights—the rights of the Unionist majority. Our quarrel has gone on for a long time. It is out of date. Its very existence is a denial of our common Christianity and it poses a serious question about our Christian commitment. As far back as the sixth century, St. Columba, a forefather of both our traditions, returned from exile in Iona to settle an earlier version of our present quarrel. But, sadly, it is still with us today. We cannot wait for another St. Columba. We now need the intervention of the rest of humanity so that we can finally heal our divisions and achieve a lasting peace.

Having cast aside sectarian differences, there will be many economic challenges ahead. The investments flowing from America and Europe, as I outlined them earlier, are hugely welcome. Indigenous enterprise will grow. The government is offering cash incentives for returning emigrants setting up in business—190,000 people have left in the past twenty-five years of violence. The key will be to make sure that the revenues are spent fairly. The fact that we can focus on a widening east–west divide within Ireland is a worrying indication that a new partition, based on economic and social structures, is in the making.

The growing concentration of population and employment in the urban sprawls of Dublin and Kildare in the Republic, and of Belfast, north Down and south Antrim in the North, is striking. The concentration of media and cultural resources is common to both the northern and southern parts of the east coast. Indeed, even the very welcome proposal for an east coast economic corridor is a recognition of the common interests of the areas east of the Bann and Shannon.

All this contrasts with the problems of the west. Twenty years ago, we thought that the type of decline charted in the wake of the Great Famine was long past. But desertification seems to have set in once more. Towns and villages are being devastated by emigration, both to the east of Ireland and further afield. Increasingly, the economically inactive old and very young predominate. The remaining agricultural population sees itself under threat from the reform of the Common Agricultural Policy (CAP) and the General Agreement on Tariffs and Trade (GATT) negotiations. The fear that the west will become a theme park for affluent tourists from the east and abroad is widespread.

The material conditions for a new partition are emerging. But, just as I would argue that the north–south political divide has been destructive for both parts of Ireland, a new socio-economic partition between east and west would be equally damaging to all our interests.

For those in the west, there is nothing to be gained from indulging in begrudgery at the expense of the east. While these things are relative, there are obviously massive problems of unemployment and deprivation to be found in the east as well.

A west kept alive on a drip feed of transfer payments would not ultimately benefit the east, either politically or economically. The tensions between a relatively affluent north and a more impoverished south have had a serious impact on both the economy and political systems of at least two of our European neighbours, Italy and Belgium. Given the existing divisions within this island, it does not seem sensible to exacerbate our problems by creating new disputes as a result of unbalanced development. Neo-classical economists may tell us that the shift to the east is inevitable, and therefore to be welcomed. However, I do not believe in the inevitability of the decline of the west. Balanced development is in our collective interests. Just as it has been accepted that the European Union has a responsibility to promote convergence between the richer and poorer member states, the respective metropolitan centres have a duty and self-interest in the welfare of all the territory under their jurisdiction.

Bringing about such balanced development requires a new model of centre–periphery relations, which I would term polycentric. The concept of peripherality is useful—it is a helpful tool of economic analysis, and serves as a foundation for any coherent strategy of balanced development—but it is also double-edged. Obviously, if decision-makers in our centres recognise the specific problems caused by geographical remoteness, they are more likely to take our interests into account. Similarly, if ministers and civil servants in Dublin, Belfast and London understand that they, given the global nature of the economy, are also someone else's periphery, they are more likely to respond sympathetically to our problems.

Perhaps paradoxically, the geographical periphery stands to gain more if the concept of peripherality forms part of the intellectual framework of the centre. Otherwise, there is a real danger that, if we in the periphery internalise the notion and come to see ourselves as culturally, politically and economically marginal, we will surrender to the "victim syndrome". If we identify ourselves as victims, alternately persecuted or neglected by the centre, we are preparing the way for a profound psychological demoralisation, and setting the stage for a capitulation to the so-called laws of economics.

The most important lesson we have learned in Derry over the last few years is that, from where we stand, we are the centre. I am not pretending that we do not have serious difficulties in our city, but most visitors seem able to detect a certain frame of mind that has resulted in Derry being one of the few expanding urban centres in the west.

The extent to which we have succeeded in regenerating this part of the west is the result of two principles. Firstly, we do not expect the centre to solve our problems, but we expect it rather to make it possible for us to resolve them ourselves. Secondly, we do not believe in monogamy in our relations with the outside world. As far as the centre is concerned, we are polygamists. Rather than put all our hopes in the Belfast or London baskets, we look for opportunities and partnerships with an entire harem of centres.

Our airport and new harbour exist primarily because of our contacts with Brussels; civil service offices have been located in the city; new investment projects have come in from California; and the International Fund for Ireland has helped to finance the restoration of the city centre. In a polycentric world, promiscuity is an advantage.

Our relationship with the rest of Europe, and the wider world, is just as important as the relationship between the various parts of Ireland, north, west, south and east. Not only must we strive to establish co-operative projects between the various corners of our island, we must also look outwards.

The image of a supplicant, downtrodden west, holding out its palms to the east, or looking to the metropolitan centres of the island for redemption, has no place in the vision of the new Ireland we must imagine and invent. That imagination, that invention, are essential if we are to guarantee, collectively, a secure future for our regions and our island.

The future will indeed be polycentric. We can see this in the institutional and geographic diversity of European structures. For example, the main EU institutions are located in Brussels, Luxembourg and Strasbourg. We look to the European Court of Human Rights in Strasbourg to uphold our fundamental freedoms. Vienna hosts the European Conference on Security and Co-operation, which does valuable work in maintaining peace in Europe. Frankfurt, it seems, is to be the home of the European Central Bank. Other common institutions are scattered throughout Europe, such as the European Bank for Reconstruction and Development in London. In Dublin, we find two headquarters of EU organisations, the Centre for the Improvement of Working Conditions and the European Bureau for Minority and Lesser Used Languages. The point is that we can no longer simply look to a unifying centre. The peripheries are multiple, and the centres diverse.

This diversity reveals itself in the increasing importance of the concept of the Europe of the Regions. The regional aspect of Union policy has gained substantially in importance since the mid-1970s, to the point where regional policy spending is the second largest item in the EU budget. Until fairly recently, however, regional policies tended to be administered by the central EU and member state institutions. The most progressive development has been the emergence of regions and local authorities as autonomous actors.

Sub-national authorities throughout the Union no longer sit back as passive recipients of largesse; they take an active role in the formulation and implementation of policies. They no longer simply address themselves to the Union authorities; they are building links between themselves, and are initiating projects and policies. In Ireland generally, we lag behind the successes of many of our German, Dutch or Belgian counterparts. There is no doubt we can all learn a great deal from the strategies other regions have adopted to overcome their natural disadvantages, just as we have much to teach.

These exchanges between regions are helping to create a network of relations, between the regions, and with the respective national capitals. From our point of view, one of the major benefits of the Maastricht Treaty is the institutional recognition which it gives to the regions in the shape of the Committee of the Regions. For the first time, the regions of Europe will be properly associated with the decision-making processes of the Union. Exactly how effective the Committee will be depends on how imaginative, responsible and self-confident its members are in putting forward proposals and policies. If it is used simply to put forward complaints, it will lose much of its credibility. In this part of Ireland, such developments have been overshadowed by the scare tactics of the British government and its alleged supporters. The Maastricht debate has been dominated by a completely false dichotomy. The British government has, so it is argued, put up a heroic fight to protect the ancient rights and freedoms of its citizens against the centralising ambitions of the Union.

Standing where we are, on the edge of Europe, being much less obsessed with the value of the nation state, and more engaged with the European mainland, this portrayal of the Union seems to have little relationship to reality. The truth is that a polycentric rather than an imperial vision is driving Europe forward. Associated with the development of multiple centres is the creation of multiple layers of identities. Simultaneously or successively, we can be Europeans, British, Irish, Northern Irish, Derrymen or Derrywomen—whatever we choose. In this new world, there are no incompatibilities between identities, there is no superiority of one identity over another, we can be free to invent ourselves. Ultimately, identity will simply become a matter of comfort and convenience, not a sign of tribal loyalty. This is the world we must seek and perhaps, invent.

I believe that such a diverse society, in which we are not confined by rigid structures or identities, has much more chance of tackling the problems of employment, environment, social justice and peace. Above all, our new polycentric world will provide a pragmatic challenge to the nineteenth-century orthodoxies which have generated the profound north–south divide and which are now in danger of creating a new and equally profound east–west barrier.

If the west is to have a future, it cannot be in hostility to the east. We must look to ourselves and to all points of the compass. In a multi-polar world, a compass is a necessity, since the traditional road signs merely point us on the road to nowhere.

The quarrel that we have in Northern Ireland is an out-of-date quarrel. To settle it will need new thinking and new ideas, because the traditional approaches have not succeeded on either side. By building new institutions which would reflect our diversity and our differences, we can end our quarrel and start working together to re-energise ourselves. Once we release all the energies and intelligence of both sections of our people into building together, rather than plotting against one another, we will really build a powerful new Ireland.

— 13 —

Ireland in a New World

I have spread my dreams under your feet.
Tread softly because you tread on my dreams.
William Butler Yeats

One of the few developments which has cheered those who believe that moderation and reason must prevail in Northern Ireland has been a growing interest in the problem on the part of responsible political leaders outside of Ireland and Britain. This is particularly true of the United States, and, to a significant extent, of the European Union.

I believe that the friends of Britain have been dismayed at evidence in recent years of a British retreat from a world view. Many have felt that this contraction of vision has been accompanied by, if it is not symptomatic of, a weakening of Britain's political psyche. That in itself, if true, should concern those who hope for a solution to Northern Ireland's problems, which, as I have argued, will require considerable political courage on the part of Britain.

Britain must be serious about the problem of Northern Ireland, a strategically placed area in the Atlantic approaches to north-west Europe, potentially ripe for subversion if political neglect were to continue. The growing unrest of American and European leaders reflects, I believe, an awareness of this threat. Several responsible American leaders have implicitly questioned Britain's capacity to meet the political challenge and, in terms of Britain's record so far in Northern Ireland, they are right to be concerned.

The interest of the West in the problem is not only strategic. History has made Ireland one of the most "internationalised" of communities in the world. The foundation of its relations with the two wings of the Western world lies in its emigration over the past centuries: in the seventeenth and eighteenth centuries to France and Spain; in the eighteenth, nineteenth and twentieth centuries to America; and again, more recently, to Britain. The basis is people: the Irish diaspora.

The situation today is intriguing: earlier links with the Continent have been renewed but now rest on the solid foundation of the treaties of the European Union. The links with America are founded on the old connections of blood, friendship and heritage, between the five million people on the island today and upwards of forty-two million people in the United States. This relationship has deepened and matured as the Republic has developed politically and economically, and as the Irish in America have prospered and built on their extraordinary political achievements of the past hundred years.

These two global relationships have played major roles in the fortunes of Ireland in recent years. From America came much of the industrial investment which created the impressive economic development of the Republic in recent years. From Europe have come the economic benefits of membership of the Union, which have transformed life, particularly in the Republic, and also created a sense of political dignity and statehood, again in the Republic, which, prior to membership, had been stifled by a claustrophobic bilateral relationship with the neighbouring island of Britain.

Since the great tides of Irish emigration began to flow to America in the nineteenth century, the Irish in America tried, without success, to interest Washington administrations in the "Irish question". Great names, such as John Devoy, editor of *The Gaelic-American*, and Éamon de Valera, were energetically involved in this endeavour, but all in vain. This is not to fault these men: it was a function of the nature of Irish political power in America at that time, which was confined to the leadership of some of the great cities and states. It remained largely excluded from Washington. That situation changed dramatically in 1961, with the Kennedy presidency.

I first met Senator Edward Kennedy in 1972. He contacted me, by telephone, and I went to meet him, and we have maintained contact ever since. Thomas P. O'Neill was the first Speaker to visit Northern Ireland and he came to visit me in Derry. Tom Foley, as Speaker, also visited Northern Ireland and my home in Derry with a major team of American Congressmen. So there has been, throughout the history of the process, a very strong Irish-American presence.

American involvement in our situation began with the work of the "four horsemen", which consisted of Thomas P. O'Neill, Governor Hugh Carey, Daniel Moynihan and Edward Kennedy. In 1977, they focused American attention on the Irish problem and on helping to solve it. Out of the four horsemen arose Friends of Ireland, a very influential body of Senators and Congressmen, and they always maintained strong contact with me.

The influence of these powerful American leaders of Irish extraction in Washington, notably Senator Edward Kennedy and then Speaker Thomas P. O'Neill, brought the issue to a point where the Carter administration adopted an initial position on Northern Ireland. As a result, the support for violence from the United States was contained and, in fact, dropped. That this should have been maintained during the past years of political vacuum in Northern Ireland is an extraordinary achievement. There are many men, women and children in Northern Ireland who are alive today, I am convinced, because of the political courage and concern of these men.

President Carter committed himself to providing economic aid in the event that a solution, acceptable to both sides in Northern Ireland, and to the British and Irish governments, could be found. That was a generous, humane and unprovocative commitment. It was welcomed by the Irish and British governments as a major incentive to reconciliation, and they were both consulted about it. The Irish question became a legitimate and serious issue in the transatlantic relationship between London and Washington.

The interest of the United States and of the European Union in Northern Ireland is historically inevitable and perfectly legitimate. This need not involve direct intervention or support for particular policies. It should be taken as encouragement—by London, by Dublin and by all parties in Northern Ireland—to have the courage to resolve this old quarrel that involves them all.

Bill Clinton put peace in Ireland uppermost on his agenda, but before his presidency we did have very strong and very valuable support from the Friends of Ireland in the Senate and in Congress. Tip O'Neill asked me what assistance should come from America in response to the Anglo-Irish Agreement. I advised him to concentrate on economic assistance. Tip, together with Senators Kennedy, Moynihan and Dodd, and Tom Foley—the Friends of Ireland—set up the International Fund for Ireland. This international fund has been very fruitful at grass roots level. There was total support throughout from the Senate and Congress, due to the influence of the Friends of Ireland.

Considering the difficulties of our past, we have got to approach the future with certain fundamental attitudes, the first being that, as we are a divided society, there cannot be any victories. There must be no banners raised high. Whatever forms of government we adopt, there must first of all be agreement. I believe we should all approach the table at which such agreement will be sought with an open mind and with no fixed views. I think we should also remember, given the nature of our problem, that the problems of the 1990s are not the problems of the 1920s. Today we see a post-Nationalist world where, in Europe in particular, we no longer have independent countries—we are, in fact, interdependent.

This fact has changed the nature of our quarrel, because, in the past, the quarrel was essentially the conflict of two nationalisms, the Irish Nationalist and the Unionist—the Unionists being, in fact, nationalists to Britain. We have to move beyond that now, because that quarrel was largely about territory, and about superiority. Nationalism, engendering imperialism, has led to some of the worst episodes in the history of the world, including two world wars. Our objective, as we look to the future, must be to embrace a completely new vision of society, not only in Ireland, but across the world.

The Irish diaspora will play an important part in this vision, if we can harness the strength and influence of people of Irish descent, from both our traditions, to assist us in the development of our island. The current revolution in modern technology, particularly in telecommunications and transportation, will be crucial to that development, and critical in terms of creating employment. However, we must realise that there is no instant solution that will resolve the problem overnight.

What we need, I say again, is a healing process, and we have to create a framework within which that healing process can take place. That framework, whether we are talking about within Northern Ireland or within Ireland as a whole, must reflect the many differences of our people and earn the allegiance and agreement of all traditions. Having created that framework, we will work together to rebuild our country, concentrating on what are our agreed common interests—social and economic development and tackling unemployment, putting bread on our tables and a roof over our heads.

By working that common ground together, we will be able to harness the energies of all our people to build, rather than to destroy, as we have done in the past. In my opinion, once we harness our energies in positive growth, we will become one of the most interesting and prosperous countries of the world.

Similarly, on north–south relations, it is quite clear that our common ground is very substantial—for example, in agriculture, tourism, the environment, fisheries. It is essential that we build institutions that will allow us to develop, by agreement, so that neither side feels threatened by the other.

The Irish are the largest group of wandering people in the world and that diaspora could bring major benefits for the development of our small island. My dream for the next century, as we approach the new millennium, is that we will have an island in which, at last, there will be no killings on our streets, and that emigration will have ended.

When our first emigrants left these shores, there was what we called an American wake. The person was as good as dead as far as the family was concerned, because they knew they would never see them again, as the distance was so great. The Irish diaspora—those people whose original roots and family are on this island—although scattered to the four corners of the earth, can now be linked together; they are only a phone call or a few hours' travel away. This is bound to lead, as has already been reflected in Europe, to the emergence of new relationships and of institutional expressions of those relationships. There need never be another American wake.

Emigration is a powerful and emotive link between ourselves and the United States. In the last census, more than forty million people took the trouble to say that they were of Irish descent. Most of the people who had to leave our island, left because of poverty and unemployment. Many of their descendants have become some of the most powerful people in the world. The Irish diaspora has spread all over the world—America, Canada, Australia, New Zealand, and throughout Europe.

We need to set in place a permanent network, drawing on their natural loyalties to the island from which their ancestors came, and with which, even today, they have a strong identity. This will bring major benefits to the island itself, in terms of providing hope for our people and ending, at last, not only the violence on our streets, but also the emigration of our young people. In unity with Irish descendants across the world, we can create a whole new concept of identity.

This may seem like a grand dream, but I believe it is a dream that can be brought into reality if we all apply our minds to it. We should recognise that, as we talk of building a new Ireland, we are doing it in the context of a new world, a much smaller place than the world at the beginning of this century.

And as we move into the next century, in that smaller world, we in Ireland, who have played such a major part in building all over the world, can give a lead in shaping that new vision and in building the links and institutions necessary to it.

In every aspect of life, economic and social philosophies have developed in the space of eighty years. It would be ludicrous to run even a corner shop today the way it was run in 1912, 1916, or 1920. Yet both the Unionist and Nationalist traditions are still based in that period and thinking. The philosophies of the 1990s are being forged in a completely different world, and we can embrace new ideas that are not based on the traditional attitudes of the past. For most of this century, both sides have been tied very much to slogans, to flag waving and to the concept of solutions which were based in conflict. Now the challenge is to build a new and a better Ireland—together.

My vision for the new century is a vision of a new Ireland, in a new Europe, in a new world. We need no longer be tied to narrow definitions of nationality or nation states, but instead we can subscribe to the knowledge that humanity can transcend nationality and that, as human beings, our major objective is to protect the basic and fundamental human rights of all our people—to include all our different traditions and identities.

We are indeed, in essence, an international people, not alone in terms of the diaspora. If we examine our own Irish roots on this island we will see that the blood of the Irish is the most diverse in the world: Milesian, Celtic, Viking, Norman, Spanish, Scottish and English. And the Irish have been travellers. From the early centuries in the days of the monks to the later Irish, many wandered the length and breadth of Europe and beyond.

One aspect of the tragic history of our island holds great potential for the future. Because of our history there is a massive Irish diaspora around the world. It is particularly significant in the United States. The Irish diaspora cuts across our ancient divide. We in Ireland take tremendous pride in the diaspora and their achievements, and they, in turn, express great pride in their Irish roots. What we must do now is harness that pride in practical terms to give back to them their ancient and original home—Ireland.

We must harness this strength in the service of peace, reconciliation and economic development in Ireland. There is no doubt that goodwill exists, there is no doubt that the potential for an active role of Irish-America in the creation of a new Ireland exists. It is up to us in Ireland and our friends in America to organise and direct the energies which are currently lying untapped. Given the technological and economic revolutions that we are living through, the world is becoming much smaller and interdependent. We all have a lot to gain by co-operation, wherever we might be.

The task that confronts us is massive. It will be difficult. Careful analysis will have to replace slogans. The challenge to all our mind-sets will be uncomfortable but absolutely necessary if Ireland is to free itself finally from the scourge of violence and poverty.

We have to look at the facts, not at the illusions. We are now at a crucial historical moment since the conditions now exist for a new Ireland—an Ireland at peace, striving to provide decent living standards for all its citizens and playing a positive role in the international community.

With the Joint Declaration of the Irish and British governments of 1993, the ceasefire of 1994 and the various proposals on the table for the political future of Ireland, there is an unprecedented opportunity to create a new Ireland.

The people of Ireland have the right to determine their future, as have all the peoples of the world. But such rights, like all rights, only pertain to people, not to territory. Without people, our planet would be a jungle. Humanity is by definition diverse. The real task of politics is to recognise our diversity and our differences, and then find ways to respect and accommodate difference. The only way to guarantee lasting stability in any society is to respect diversity.

The people of Ireland are divided over the way in which their right to self-determination should be exercised. We have to find a method by which these differences over the political direction of our country can be reconciled. We have to work towards agreement. Agreement cannot be secured by any form of violence or coercion. Neither can it be avoided by pretending agreement is not necessary, nor by thinking in terms of defeat or victory. Victories are not solutions, they simply pave the way for further conflict.

The divisions in Ireland have been intensified rather than created by the political partition of our island. Our divisions are much older than partition. We, of all political persuasions, have yet to face up to the challenge of reaching agreement between ourselves. That challenge is now openly on the agenda of the Irish and British governments and of all the political parties in Ireland, north and south.

The present political climate allows us to face up to the challenge in a serious way for the first time. The British government has made it clear that it has no selfish or strategic interest in Ireland. It has made it clear that it is not interested in upholding or imposing any form of government, including the status quo, which does not have the support of all the people. Its primary interest, in the words of the Joint Declaration is "to see peace, stability and reconciliation established by agreement among all the people who inhabit the island. The British government agree that it is for the people of the island of Ireland alone, by agreement between the two parts respectively, to exercise their right of self-determination on the basis of consent, freely and concurrently given, north and south, to bring about a united Ireland, if that is their wish. It reaffirms as a binding obligation that they will, for their part, introduce the necessary legislation to give effect to this, or equally to any measure of agreement on future relationships in Ireland which the people living in Ireland may themselves freely so determine without external impediment."

It is up to everyone in Ireland, and everyone concerned for the future, to work to secure that agreement, leaving aside traditional and outdated mind-sets and abandoning all forms of coercion and force. In practical terms, when a people like ours is divided, then every section of it has a veto on progress. We have to stop thinking in negative terms, we have to stop seeing our political opponents as enemies to be vanquished. Instead, we have to be positive. We have to sit down with people of very different views and find an agreement which suits us all. Such an agreement can only be possible if we respect our different heritages and identities and start the search for a way of protecting the rights of all sections of our people. We cannot have a stable society if any significant section of the people feel they are the losers.

The Joint Declaration of 1993 is once again very apposite. The British government committed itself to "encourage, facilitate and enable the achievement of such agreement over a period through a process of dialogue and co-operation based on full respect for the rights and identities of both traditions in Ireland." Both governments and all the political parties must now do everything they can to fulfill this ambitious agenda. The citizens of the new century will not easily forgive if those in positions of power and responsibility today do not create the foundations of a new Ireland for the new century.

Afterword

Afterword

The time has come to leave the past behind
and let history be its judge.

John Hume

A lasting peace and agreement on the future of our political institutions is still within our grasp. Of that I have no doubt. There is a great responsibility on the present generation of political leaders to resolve our conflict and ensure that it is not inherited by future generations.

Even the most blinkered politicians and paramilitaries are aware that the desire for peace is shared by the people north and south, by Unionist and Nationalist, as well as by Irish communities throughout the world. It is the duty of politicians of all persuasions to ensure that this overwhelming desire for peace is fulfilled.

The seventeen months between September 1994 and February 1996 gave us a glimpse of what "normal" life could be like. Public reaction to President Clinton's visit to Ireland was spectacular evidence of the new sense of optimism. While the aspiration for peace had been widespread for a long time, people now realise what the absence of violence could mean—the possibility of living without fear, the development of our economic potential and the opportunity to address the socio-economic problems of our society. The ceasefires have also allowed a wider political debate to develop. Other serious issues have emerged on the political agenda, issues which were masked for so long by constitutional and security problems.

I am absolutely convinced that the political conditions which made the ceasefires possible in the first place still exist.

Nothing has changed the undeniable reality that force, from whatever quarter, can only perpetuate, not resolve, the conflict. Since no one can attain their objectives by violent means, its use is futile. It is obvious that the Republican movement cannot achieve its goals by force, and neither can it be suppressed by force.

It is the prime duty of every political leader in these islands to repeat over and over again that the only way to solve the conflict is through negotiation and agreement. It is our duty to recognise, advocate and uphold the principle that there can be no victories or defeats for any one section of society. There can only be a collective and mutual victory through establishing a lasting peace and agreement on future political arrangements. Peace is the only real victory on offer, and peace is indivisible.

All of us have a responsibility to bring about that mutual victory. By all of us, I mean governments, political parties and the people. If peace is to be permanent, it can only come about through the will and determination of the ordinary citizens of these islands. The strength and the expression of the public desire for peace will be a major factor in the ultimate success of the peace process. Peace must be the people's peace.

Political parties in particular must respond to the wish of their supporters for peace. They must also take extreme care not to create more barriers to the eventual negotiated settlement which we all know is the only way forward. We have to measure the impact of our words and our actions very carefully. At the same time, we have to engage in positive confidence-building measures, such as addressing the economic and social agenda, which would benefit everyone. Mutual co-operation on these issues would not involve any surrender of identity or allegiance. It would build the trust that will assist us in the more difficult political processes.

Those of us engaged in politics also have a duty to be imaginative. It is not enough to repeat the old doctrines in a vain attempt to offer traditional forms of reassurance to our supporters. Neither can we resort to the lazy thinking involved in importing faded orthodoxies from elsewhere. We have to tell people the truth, however uncomfortable it may be. All political parties need to analyse individually and collectively the new world in which we find ourselves. We must look at the reality of our divisions and conduct an audit of the various traditions in order to decide which aspects are worthy of preservation and which would better be consigned to a museum. The same process of analysis and modernisation must also be applied to relationships between Unionists and Nationalists, between north and south and between Britain and both parts of Ireland.

Furthermore, relations between Britain, Ireland and the rest of the world have an important bearing on the relations between the two countries themselves. The two islands, although one is much larger than the other, are drops in the global ocean and are undergoing profound transformations in their relations with the international community. The implications of such changes are not yet fully visible.

It is also essential to realise that the conflict in Ireland does not take place in a vacuum. The economic and technological changes in the world economy have as much impact on the welfare of our citizens as the political conflict. We need to identify the steps which must be taken so that we can face the future with anticipation rather than trepidation. We need to look outward and forward, rather than wallow in an introspective obsession with the past.

Finally, it is up to political leaders to prove that the political process works. Resolving our divisions can only be accomplished by serious all-inclusive negotiation, conducted in good faith by all parties. This process will, naturally, involve substantial disagreement, tactical manoeuvring and periodic crises. No one pretends that finding agreement will be easy. But it is essential that the negotiators, while arguing their respective cases as vigorously as possible, pursue their work with their eyes fixed on the ultimate aim of securing agreement. If all parties to the conflict want an agreement, then I am convinced it will eventually be found.

Such an agreement demands that everyone involved should place the emphasis on what they stand for, rather than what they are against. By now, everyone is tired of hearing what the various parties are against.

For constitutional nationalism, there is a need to acknowledge that the traditionally-conceived nation-state has always been an aspiration rather than a reality in our country. The state has not been co-terminous with the nation, not simply because of the existence of a border across the island but also because millions of our people have left Ireland over the last 150 years.

Many, from both traditions, have retained a sense of identity with their island homeland. They still regard themselves as part of the Irish nation. In today's smaller world, we can and should give a positive expression to that identity and translate it into a concept of political organisation which accommodates the different traditions on our island and which embraces, and makes use of, the diaspora. The task now is to devise a settlement which guarantees the identity and status of everyone in Ireland, irrespective of politics, as well as everyone who is Irish, irrespective of geography. Naturally, the arrangements must have the loyalty and involvement of both traditions.

It is impossible to ignore the profound social and economic changes of the last three decades. The whole of Ireland is now a far more urbanised society with a highly-educated population. The consequences can be seen in the increasingly pluralist nature of society, in the decline of automatic allegiance to a political party, in the increased relevance of socio-economic issues and openness towards the European Union and our European partners.

Yet political structures have not evolved to reflect the diversity of, and changes in, society. Ireland, both in the north and the south, is governed in a highly centralist fashion, more appropriate to an era when education and administrative skills were confined to a small élite. It is significant that the degree of centralisation in both jurisdictions is intimately connected with the failure to find a consensus throughout Ireland on suitable forms of government and indeed to our failure to achieve maximum economic development.

Nationalist Ireland must ensure that no significant section of society can feel itself threatened by the imposition of structures, policies and values which do not take into account its legitimate interests and aspirations. This is essential if Nationalists are to prove that their ideal is one of inclusion and openness, rather than exclusion and separatism. We have to prove that the concepts of Ireland and an Irish identity are not hostile or threatening to the Unionist tradition. Much of the credibility of the Nationalist tradition in the eyes of those who do not share its assumptions will therefore depend on the way the diversity within Nationalist Ireland itself is accommodated.

The Republican movement must also continue the process of re-examining its traditional attitudes. 1996 is not 1916. It knows that it cannot achieve justice for the communities it represents through the use of force. It is essential that it become part of the mainstream of politics in Ireland and elsewhere. However, it cannot do so unless it is prepared to guarantee that it is committed exclusively to dialogue and peaceful persuasion as its means of resolving the conflict.

The ending of the marginalisation and exclusion of the Republican movement and its supporters lies now, to a significant extent, in its own hands. Although it is obvious that there are some politicians in Ireland and Britain who have a positive desire to maintain the exclusion of Republicans, their importance is a temporary phenomenon occasioned by the arithmetic of Westminster. The vast majority of democratic politicians in these islands now accept that Republicans must be part of the solution. It is up to Republicans to persuade everyone that they want to be part of that solution.

Many Republicans would claim that they have already demonstrated their commitment to the search for peace. Although I do not doubt their sincerity, or dismiss their fears about the intentions of their political opponents, they must accept that other parties have their worries about Republican intentions. No one can expect trust to be spontaneously given or easily established, but fear cannot be allowed to block political progress. Republicans must therefore understand that their credibility in the eyes of those with whom they wish to negotiate is greatly undermined by the continuation of, and the potential to carry on, the armed campaign. Sooner or later, Republicans will have to resolve this problem themselves if they are not to substantially contribute to their own exclusion from the political process.

There are some who see the overwhelming support for peace as a weapon to be used against the Republican movement. This would be a great mistake. Peace campaigns which, in the past, attempted to pin the blame for the conflict on one side or the other were short-lived and doomed to failure. Peace cannot be construed as a victory of one side over another. Peace can only be established if everyone believes that a just settlement has been reached. The onus is on Republicans to build on the support for peace and to campaign peacefully for the type of political changes which almost everyone agrees are necessary and possible. The absence of violence would provide Republicans with the opportunity to establish new political institutions, taking into account the interests and aspirations of all the people of our divided Ireland.

Republicans need to intensify their analysis of the contradictions in their present strategy and to recognise, once and for all, that the crucial issue in Irish politics is changing hearts and minds, not redrawing lines on the map. They will have to recognise that the contemporary world is much more complex than the one which confronted the founders of their movement and that traditions only survive and prosper through their ability to adapt to change. Much progress has been made but not enough, so far, to ensure a peaceful resolution of the conflict. The proof is in the fact that the cessation of violence of 1994 ended in what can only be described as the major political defeat of February 1996.

Nationalist Ireland has to reassure Unionists that it is interested in coming to an agreement with them, rather than in absorbing them or otherwise denying their distinct identity. But, equally, we have a right to expect of Unionists that they demonstrate their support for such an agreement, rather than conduct vain attempts to maintain their supremacy or barricade themselves inside an outdated and self-deluding laager. Northern Ireland cannot insulate itself from the wider world, and especially not from its nearest neighbours. Neither can the two traditions in Northern Ireland live apart from each other, nor one thrive at the expense of the other. Unfortunately, Nationalists have yet to be convinced that Unionist leaders understand these realities.

Just as Nationalists and Republicans have to come to terms with the inadequacies of their past assumptions, so do Unionists. A great deal of serious thinking is going on within unionism, but this is not reflected in the pronouncements of mainstream Unionist leaders. The challenge for Unionists and their leaders is to produce a modern statement of their ideals, their legitimate interests and their aspirations. While it is obviously up to Unionists themselves to produce such a statement, one crucial aspect would be the definition of the relationship with Nationalist Ireland, north and south. Unionist would-be modernisers who try to pretend that all that matters is their relationship with the UK are missing the real point. It makes no political or economic sense to attempt to ignore the Irish dimension as some of the theoreticians of modern unionism seem to believe.

It would be in the interest of all the peoples of these islands if unionism was to transform itself into a forward-looking and confident political movement, capable of articulating a positive vision of its own, reflecting the realities of the society in which it exists. A defensive and insecure unionism does us all a disservice. Such insecurity is a major inhibiting factor. On the socio-economic front, the number of young people from the Unionist tradition who leave Northern Ireland for their higher education and never return should be a serious source of concern to both Unionists and Nationalists. The ultimate implications for the future of Northern Ireland's economy are obvious. Unionist insecurity also hinders the process of negotiating an eventual agreement, since no one likes to negotiate from a position of weakness.

Unionism is, and will continue to be, an integral feature of the Irish political landscape. That is a fact guaranteed not so much by British constitutional theory as by the history, geography and politics of the Unionist community itself, which is its real strength and its real security. It is also reinforced by the acceptance by the vast majority of today's Nationalists that the Unionist identity in Ireland is distinct and legitimate. Historically speaking, this is a very new development. A historic opportunity exists for Unionists to finally establish the security in Ireland for which they have craved for centuries. That can only be done by agreement and ensuring parity of esteem between our two traditions. It would be criminal to waste such an opportunity.

The British government are fond of reminding everyone that they are the sovereign authority in Northern Ireland. This claim to sovereignty would have been less controversial if, over the years, they had displayed as much commitment to resolving the divisions in our society as to making resounding declarations of their responsibility to do so. However, much progress has been made in recent years as the conflict in Ireland has pushed its way up the political agenda and governments have made some serious efforts to deal with it.

But much remains to be done. In December 1993, the British government signed the Downing Street Declaration committing themselves to working for an agreement among the divided people of Ireland. However, there is a widespread perception that they have not really lived up to this promise. The various obstacles to all-party talks which have emerged since August 1994 have not inspired confidence in the determination of the British government to promote a negotiated settlement. This has damaged the peace process, but it is not too late to put the peace process back on track.

This is not to deny that the British government may sometimes have to take decisions which one or more parties dislike. Nor is it to suggest that they can impose a solution. But they do have a duty to keep sight of the ultimate objective of an agreed settlement, to push the peace process along and to avoid adopting the agenda of one party over another. They have the power to impress upon all parties the necessity of engaging in serious negotiations and the signals they send out have a substantial impact on the willingness of those parties to do so—there must be no reward for evasiveness and intransigence. They must help to build the confidence needed to get everyone around the negotiating table.

It would also be a mistake for the British government to adopt the complacent attitude that, if all the parties involved are more or less dissatisfied with their policies, then they are doing well. Unfortunately, this is the advice of some of the more superficial commentators. Quite apart from the patronising and stereotypical undertones of such an attitude, it betrays a sad lack of ambition. Surely any British government, whatever their political complexion, should be aiming to win a positive agreement between the different parties to the conflict.

Peace is possible, but it is by no means certain. Resolving centuries of conflict will inevitably be a long process. It is urgent, therefore, that we delay no longer, but begin the process of reconciliation now.

We all have to have the moral courage to seize this opportunity. It is clearly going to take time and effort to arrive at an agreement. No instant package will wipe away the damage done over the centuries. But I am absolutely certain that agreement will eventually emerge. The healing process must begin. The old prejudices and hatreds will progressively dissolve. The new Ireland of the twenty-first century will emerge out of that process. It will not, in all likelihood, conform to any of our traditional models. It will be an Ireland based on respect for diversity rather than devotion to homogeneity. The twenty-first century will be a post-nationalist and interdependent world. Through our own efforts and the support of our friends throughout the world, Catholic, Protestant and Dissenter will come together on our small island and at last the gun will have no role in the politics of our land.

Anglo-Irish Agreement 1985

Agreement between The Government of Ireland and The Government of the United Kingdom

The Government of Ireland and the Government of the United Kingdom:

Wishing further to develop the unique relationship between their peoples and the close co-operation between their countries as friendly neighbours and as partners in the European Community;

Recognising the major interest of both their countries and, above all, of the people of Northern Ireland in diminishing the divisions there and achieving lasting peace and stability;

Recognising the need for continuing efforts to reconcile and to acknowledge the rights of the two major traditions that exist in Ireland, represented on the one hand by those who wish for no change in the present status of Northern Ireland and on the other hand by those who aspire to a sovereign united Ireland achieved by peaceful means and through agreement;

Reaffirming their total rejection of any attempt to promote political objectives by violence or the threat of violence and their determination to work together to ensure that those who adopt or support such methods do not succeed;

Recognising that a condition of genuine reconciliation and dialogue between unionists and nationalists is mutual recognition and acceptance of each other's rights;

Recognising and respecting the identities of the two communities in Northern Ireland, and the right of each to pursue its aspirations by peaceful and constitutional means;

Reaffirming their commitment to a society in Northern Ireland in which all may live in peace, free from discrimination and intolerance, in the structures and processes of government;

Have accordingly agreed as follows:

A *Status of Northern Ireland*

Article 1

The two Governments

(a) affirm that any change in the status of Northern Ireland would only come about with the consent of a majority of the people of Northern Ireland;

(b) recognise that the present wish of a majority of the people of Northern Ireland is for no change in the status of Northern Ireland;

(c) declare that, if in the future a majority of the people of Northern Ireland clearly wish for and formally consent to the establishment of a united Ireland, they will introduce and support in the respective Parliaments legislation to give effect to that wish.

B *The Intergovernmental Conference*

Article 2

(a) There is hereby established, within the framework of the Anglo-Irish Intergovernmental Council set up after the meeting between the two Heads of Government on 6 November 1981, an Intergovernmental Conference (hereinafter referred to as "the Conference"), concerned with Northern Ireland and with relations between the two parts of the island of Ireland, to deal, as set out in this Agreement, on a regular basis with

- (i) political matters;
- (ii) security and related matters;
- (iii) legal matters, including the administration of justice;
- (iv) the promotion of cross-border co-operation.

(b) The United Kingdom Government accept that the Irish Government will put forward views and proposals on matters relating to Northern Ireland within the field of activity of the Conference in so far as those matters are not the responsibility of a devolved administration in Northern Ireland. In the interest of promoting peace and stability , determined efforts shall be made through the Conference to resolve any difference. The Conference will be mainly concerned with Northern Ireland; but some of the matters under consideration will involve co-operative action in both parts of the island of Ireland, and possibly also in Great Britain. Some of the proposals considered in respect of Northern Ireland may also be found to have application by the Irish Government. There is no derogation from the sovereignty of either the Irish Government or the United Kingdom Government, and each retains responsibility for the decisions and administration of government within its own jurisdiction.

Article 3

The Conference shall meet at Ministerial or official level, as required. The business of the Conference will thus receive attention at the highest level. Regular and frequent Ministerial meetings shall be held; and in particular special meetings shall be convened at the request of either side. Officials may meet in subordinate groups. Membership of the Conference and of sub-groups shall be small and flexible. When the Conference meets at Ministerial level and Irish Minister designated as the Permanent Irish Ministerial Representative and the Secretary of State for Northern Ireland shall be joint Chairmen. Within the framework of the Conference other Irish and British Ministers may hold or attend meetings as appropriate: when legal matters are under consideration the Attorneys General may attend. Ministers may be accompanied by their officials and their professional advisers: for example, when questions of security policy or security co-operation are being discussed, they may be accompanied by the Commissioner of the Garda Síochána and the Chief Constable of the Royal Ulster Constabulary; or when questions of economic or social policy or co-operation are being discussed, they may be accompanied by officials of the relevant Departments. A Secretariat shall be established by the two Governments to service the Conference on a continuing basis in the discharge of its functions as set out in this Agreement.

Article 4

(a) In relation to matters coming within its field of activity, the Conference shall be a framework within which the Irish Government and the United Kingdom Government work together

  (i) for the accommodation of the rights and identities of the two traditions which exist in Northern Ireland; and

  (ii) for peace, stability and prosperity throughout the island of Ireland by promoting reconciliation, respect for human rights, co-operation against terrorism and the development of economic, social and cultural co-operation.

(b) It is the declared policy of the United Kingdom Government that responsibility in respect of certain matters within the powers of the Secretary of State for Northern Ireland should be devolved within Northern Ireland on a basis which would secure widespread acceptance throughout the community. The Irish Government support that policy.

(c) Both Governments recognise that devolution can be achieved only with the co-operation of constitutional representatives within

Northern Ireland of both traditions there. The Conference shall be a framework within which the Irish Government may put forward views and proposals on the modalities of bringing about devolution in Northern Ireland, in so far as they relate to the interests of the minority community.

C *Political Matters*

Article 5

(a) The Conference shall concern itself with measures to recognise and accommodate the rights and identities of the two traditions in Northern Ireland, to protect human rights and to prevent discrimination. Matters to be considered in this area include measures to foster the cultural heritage of both traditions, changes in electoral arrangements, the use of flags and emblems, the avoidance of economic and social discrimination and the advantages and disadvantages of a Bill of Rights in some form in Northern Ireland.

(b) The discussion of these matters shall be mainly concerned with Northern Ireland, but the possible application of any measures pursuant to this Article by the Irish Government in their jurisdiction shall not be excluded.

(c) If it should prove impossible to achieve and sustain devolution on a basis which secures widespread acceptance in Northern Ireland, the Conference shall be a framework within which the Irish Government may, where the interest of the minority community are significantly or especially affected, put forward views on proposals for major legislation and on major policy issues, which are within the purview of the Northern Ireland Departments and which remain the responsibility of the Secretary of State for Northern Ireland.

Article 6

The Conference shall be a framework within which the Irish Government nay put forward views and proposals on the role and composition of bodies appointed by the Secretary of State for Northern Ireland or by Departments subject to his direction and control including

the Standing Advisory Commission on Human Rights;
the Fair Employment Agency;
the Equal Opportunities Commission;
the Police Authority for Northern Ireland;
the Police Complaints Board.

D *Security and Related Matters*

Article 7

(a) The Conference shall consider

(i) security policy;

(ii) relations between the security forces and the community;

(iii) prisons policy.

(b) The Conference shall consider the security situation at its regular meetings and thus provide an opportunity to address policy issues, serious incidents and forthcoming events.

(c) The two Governments agree that there is a need for a programme of special measures in Northern Ireland to improve relations between the security forces and the community, with the object in particular of making the security forces more readily accepted by the nationalist community. Such a programme shall be developed, for the Conference's consideration , and may include the establishment of local consultative machinery, training in community relations, crime prevention schemes involving the community, improvements in arrangements for handling complaints, and action to increase the proportion of members of the minority in the Royal Ulster Constabulary. Elements of the programme may be considered by the Irish Government suitable for application within their jurisdiction.

(d) The Conference may consider policy issues relating to prisons. Individual cases may be raised as appropriate, so that information can be provided or inquiries instituted.

E *Legal Matters, Including the Administration of Justice*

Article 8

The Conference shall deal with issues of concern to both countries relating to the enforcement of the criminal law. In particular it shall consider whether there are areas of the criminal law applying in the North and in the South respectively which might with benefit be harmonised. The two Governments agree on the importance of public confidence in the administration of justice. The Conference shall seek, with the help of advice from experts as appropriate, measures which would give substantial expression to this aim, considering inter alia the possibility of mixed courts in both jurisdictions for the trial of certain offences. The Conference shall also be concerned with policy aspects of extradition and extra-territorial jurisdiction as between North and South.

F *Cross-border Co-operation on Security, Economic, Social and Cultural Matters*

Article 9

(a) With a view to enhancing cross-border co-operation on security matters, the Conference shall set in hand a programme of work to be undertaken by the Commissioner of the Garda Síochána and the Chief Constable of the Royal Ulster Constabulary and, where appropriate, groups of officials, in such areas as threat assessments, exchange of information, liaison strictures, technical co-operation, training of personnel, and operational resources.

(b) The Conference shall have no operational responsibilities; responsibility for police operations shall remain with the heads of the respective police forces, the Commissioner of the Garda Síochána maintaining his links with the Minister for Justice and the Chief Constable of the Royal Ulster Constabulary his links with the Secretary of State for Northern Ireland.

Article 10

(a) The two Governments shall co-operate to promote the economic and social development of those area of both parts of Ireland which have suffered most severely from the consequences of the instability of recent years, and shall consider the possibility of securing international support for this work.

(b) If it should prove impossible to achieve and sustain devolution on a basis which secures widespread acceptance in Northern Ireland, the Conference shall be a framework for the promotion of co-operation between the two parts of Ireland concerning cross-border aspects of economic, social and cultural matters in relation to which the Secretary of State for Northern Ireland continues to exercise authority.

(c) If responsibility is devolved in respect of certain matters in the economic, social or cultural areas currently within the responsibility of the Secretary of State for Northern Ireland, machinery will need to be established by the responsible authorities in the North and South for practical co-operation in respect of cross-border aspects of these issues.

G *Arrangements for Review*

Article 11

At the end of three years from signature of this Agreement, or earlier if requested by either Government, the working of the Conference shall be reviewed by the two Governments to see whether any changes in the scope and nature of its activities are desirable.

H *Interparliamentary Relations*

Article 12

It will be for Parliamentary decision in Dublin and in Westminster whether to establish an Anglo-Irish Parliamentary body of the kind adumbrated in the Anglo-Irish Studies Report of November 1981. The two Governments agree that they would give support as appropriate to such a body, of it were to be established.

I *Final Clauses*

Article 13

This Agreement shall enter into force on the date on which the two Governments exchange notifications of their acceptance of this Agreement.

Joint Declaration 1993

Message from the Government

This Joint Declaration is a charter for peace and reconciliation in Ireland. Peace is a very simple, but also a very powerful idea, whose time has come. The Joint Declaration provides from everyone's point of view a noble means of establishing the first step towards a lasting peace in Ireland.

The central idea behind the Peace Declaration is that the problems of Northern Ireland, however deep and intractable, however difficult to reconcile, have to be resolved exclusively by political and democratic means. Its objective is to heal divisions among the peoples of Ireland.

The Declaration makes it clear that it is for the people of Ireland, North and South, to achieve agreement without outside impediment. The British Government have also declared that they will encourage, enable and facilitate such an agreement, and that they will endorse whatever agreement emerges and take the necessary steps to implement it. The language of the Declaration quite clearly makes both Governments persuaders for agreement between the people of Ireland.

The dynamic for future progress must reside in the full use of the democratic political process, in the underlying changes in Irish society, North and South, and in our external environment.

Peace is the first essential for better relationships on this island. The Joint Declaration is only the first stage in the Peace Process. There will never be a better opportunity. Peace will allow us to develop a new atmosphere of trust and co-operation and to establish a new era of *détente*, which is the only way forward.

Joint Declaration

1 The Taoiseach, Mr. Albert Reynolds, TD and the Prime Minister, the Rt. Hon. John Major MP, acknowledge that the most urgent and important issue facing the people of Ireland, North and South, and the British and Irish Governments together, is to remove the conflict, to overcome the legacy of history and to heal the divisions which have resulted, recognising the absence of a lasting and satisfactory settlement of relationships between the peoples of both islands has contributed to continuing tragedy and suffering. They believe that the development of an agreed framework for peace, which has been discussed between them since

early last year, and which is based on a number of key principles articulated by the two Governments over the past 20 years, together with the adaptation of other widely accepted principles, provides the starting point of a peace process designed to culminate in a political settlement.

2 The Taoiseach and the Prime Minister are convinced of the inestimable value to both their peoples, and particularly for the next generation, of healing divisions in Ireland and of ending a conflict which has been so manifestly to the detriment of all. Both recognise that the ending of divisions can come about only through the agreement and co-operation of the people, North and South, representing both traditions in Ireland. They therefore make a solemn commitment to promote co-operation at all levels on the basis of the fundamental principles, undertakings, obligations under international agreements, to which they have jointly committed themselves, and the guarantees which each Government has given and now reaffirms, including Northern Ireland's statutory constitutional guarantee. It is their aim to foster agreement and reconciliation, leading to a new political framework founded on consent and encompassing arrangements within Northern Ireland, for the whole island, and between these islands.

3 They also consider that the development of Europe will, of itself, require new approaches to serve interests common to both parts of the island of Ireland, and to Ireland and the United Kingdom as partners in the European Union.

4 The Prime Minister, on behalf of the British Government, reaffirms that they will uphold the democratic wish of the greater number of the people of Northern Ireland on the issue of whether they prefer to support the Union or a sovereign united Ireland. On this basis, he reiterates, on the behalf of the British Government, that they have no selfish strategic or economic interest in Northern Ireland. Their primary interest is to see peace, stability and reconciliation established by agreement among all the people who inhabit the island, and they will work together with the Irish Government to achieve such an agreement, which will embrace the totality of relationships. The role of the British Government will be to encourage, facilitate and enable the achievement of such agreement over a period through a process of dialogue and co-operation based on full respect for the rights and identities of both traditions in Ireland. They accept that such agreement may, as of right, take the form of agreed structures for the island as a whole, including a united Ireland achieved by peaceful means on the following basis. The British Government agree that it is for the people of the island of Ireland alone, by agreement between the two parts respectively, to exercise their right of self-determination on the basis of consent, freely and concurrently given, North and South, to bring about a united Ireland, if that

is their wish. They reaffirm as a binding obligation that they will, for their part, introduce the necessary legislation to give effect to this, or equally to any measure of agreement on future relationships in Ireland which the people living in Ireland may themselves freely so determine without external impediment. They believe that the people of Britain would wish, in friendship to all sides, to enable the people of Ireland to reach agreement on how they may live together in harmony and in partnership, with respect for their diverse traditions, and with full recognition of the special links and the unique relationship which exist between the peoples of Britain and Ireland.

5 The Taoiseach, on behalf of the Irish Government, considers that the lessons of Irish history, and especially of Northern Ireland, show that stability and well-being will not be found under any political system which is refused allegiance or rejected on grounds of identity by a significant minority of those governed by it. For this reason, it would be wrong to attempt to impose a united Ireland, in the absence of the freely given consent of the majority of the people of Northern Ireland. He accepts, on behalf of the Irish Government, that the democratic right of self-determination by the people of Ireland as a whole must be achieved and exercised with and subject to the agreement and consent of a majority of the people of Northern Ireland and must, consistent with justice and equity, respect the democratic dignity and the civil rights and religious liberties of both communities, including:

the right of free political thought;

the right of freedom and expression of religion;

the right to pursue democratically national and political aspirations;

the right to seek constitutional change by peaceful and legitimate means;

the right to live wherever one chooses without hindrance;

the right to equal opportunity in all social and economic activity, regardless of class, creed, sex or colour.

These would be reflected in any future political and constitutional arrangements emerging from a new and more broadly based agreement.

6 The Taoiseach however recognises the genuine difficulties and barriers to building relationships of trust either within or beyond Northern Ireland, from which both traditions suffer. He will work to create a new era of trust, in which suspicion of the motives and actions of others is removed on the part of either community. He considers that the future of the island depends on the nature of the relationship between the two main traditions that inhabit it. Every effort must be made to build a new sense of trust between those communities. In recognition of the fears of

the Unionist community and as a token of his willingness to make a political contribution to the building up of that necessary trust, the Taoiseach will examine with his colleagues any elements in the democratic life and organisation of the Irish State that can be represented to the Irish Government in the course of political dialogue as a real and substantial threat to their way of life and ethos, or that can be represented as not being fully consistent with a modern democratic and pluralist society, and undertakes to examine any possible ways of removing such obstacles. Such an examination would of course have due regard to the desire to preserve those inherited values that are largely shared throughout the island or that belong to the cultural and historical roots of the people of this island in all their diversity. The Taoiseach hopes that over time a meeting of hearts and minds will develop, which will bring all the people of Ireland together, and will work towards that objective, but he pledges in the meantime that as a result of the efforts that will be made to build mutual confidence no Northern Unionist should ever have a fear in future that this ideal will be pursued either by threat or coercion.

7 Both Governments accept that Irish unity would be achieved only by those who favour this outcome persuading those who do not, peacefully and without coercion or violence, and that, if in the future a majority of the people of Northern Ireland are so persuaded, both Governments will support and give legislative effect to their wish. But, notwithstanding the solemn affirmation by both Governments in the Anglo-Irish Agreement that any change in the status of Northern Ireland, would only come about with a consent of the majority of the people of Northern Ireland, the Taoiseach also recognises the continuing uncertainties and misgivings which dominate so much of Northern Unionist attitudes towards the rest of Ireland. He believes that we stand at a stage of our history when the genuine feelings of all traditions in the North must be recognised and acknowledged. He appeals to both traditions at this time to grasp the opportunity for a fresh start and a new beginning, which could hold such promise for all our lives and the generations to come. He asks the people of Northern Ireland to look on the people of the Republic as friends, who share their grief and shame over all the suffering of the last quarter of a century, and who want to develop the best possible relationship with them, a relationship in which trust and new understanding can flourish and grow. The Taoiseach also acknowledges the presence in the Constitution of the Republic of elements which are deeply resented by Northern Unionists, but which at the same time reflect hopes and ideals which lie deep in the hearts of many Irish men and women North and South. But as we move towards a new era of understanding in which new relationships of trust may grow and bring peace to the island of Ireland, the Taoiseach believes that the time has come to consider

together how best the hopes and identities of all can be expressed in more balanced ways, which no longer engender division and the lack of trust to which he has referred. He confirms that, in the event of an overall settlement, the Irish Government will, as part of a balanced constitutional accommodation, put forward and support proposals for change in the Irish Constitution which would fully reflect the principle of consent in Northern Ireland.

8 The Taoiseach recognises the need to engage in dialogue which would address with honesty and integrity the fears of all traditions. But that dialogue, both within the North and between the people and their representatives of both parts of Ireland, must be entered into with an acknowledgment that the future security and welfare of the people of the island will depend on an open, frank and balanced approach to all the problems which for too long have caused division.

9 The British and Irish Governments will seek, along with the Northern Ireland constitutional parties through a process of political dialogue, to create institutions and structures which, while respecting the diversity of the people of Ireland, would enable them to work together in all areas of common interest. This will help over a period to build the trust necessary to end past divisions, leading to an agreed and peaceful future. Such structures would, of course, include institutional recognition of the special links that exist between the peoples of Britain and Ireland as part of the totality of relationships, while taking account of newly forged links with the rest of Europe.

10 The British and Irish Governments reiterate that the achievement of peace must involve a permanent end to the use of, or support for, paramilitary violence. They confirm that, in these circumstances, democratically mandated parties which establish a commitment to exclusively peaceful methods and which have shown that they abide by the democratic process, are free to participate fully in democratic politics and to join in dialogue in due course between the Governments and the political parties on the way ahead.

11 The Irish Government would make their own arrangements within their jurisdiction to enable democratic parties to consult together and share in dialogue about the political future. The Taoiseach's intention is that these arrangements could include the establishment, in consultation with other parties, of a Forum for Peace and Reconciliation to make recommendations on ways in which agreement and trust between both traditions can be promoted and established.

12 The Taoiseach and the Prime Minister are determined to build on the fervent wish of both their peoples to see old fears and anomalies replaced by a climate of peace. They believe the framework

they have set out offers the people of Ireland, North and South, whatever their tradition, the basis to agree that from now on their differences can be negotiated and resolved exclusively by peaceful political means. They appeal to all concerned to grasp the opportunity for a new departure. That step would compromise no position or principle, nor prejudice the future of either community. On the contrary, it would be an incomparable gain for all. It would break decisively the cycle of violence and the intolerable suffering it entails for the people of these islands, particularly for both communities in Northern Ireland. It would allow the process of economic and social co-operation on the island to realise its full potential for prosperity and mutual understanding. It would transform the prospects for building on the progress already made in the Talks process, involving the two Governments and the constitutional parties in Northern Ireland. The Taoiseach and the Prime Minister believe that these arrangements offer an opportunity to lay the foundation for a more peaceful and harmonious future, devoid of the violence and bitter divisions which have scarred the past generation. They commit themselves and their Governments to continue to work together, unremittingly, towards that objective.

Framework Document 1995

A New Framework for Agreement

A shared understanding between the British and Irish Governments to assist discussion and negotiation involving the Northern Ireland parties

1 The Joint Declaration acknowledges that the most urgent and important issue facing the people of Ireland, North and South, and the British and Irish Governments together, is to remove the causes of conflict, to overcome the legacy of history and to heal the divisions which have resulted.

2 Both Governments recognise that there is much cause for deep regret on all sides in the long and often tragic history of Anglo-Irish relations, and of relations in Ireland. They believe it is now time to lay aside, with dignity and forbearance, the mistakes of the past. A collective effort is needed to create, through agreement and reconciliation, a new beginning, founded on consent, for relationships within Northern Ireland, within the island of Ireland and between the peoples of these islands. The Joint Declaration itself represents an important step towards this goal, offering the people of Ireland, North and South, whatever their tradition, the basis to agree that from now on their differences can be negotiated and resolved exclusively by peaceful political means.

3 The announcements made by the Irish Republican Army on 31 August 1994 and the Combined Loyalist Military Command on 13 October 1994 are a welcome response to the profound desire of people throughout these islands for a permanent end to the violence which caused such immense suffering and waste and served only to reinforce the barriers of fear and hatred, impeding the search for agreement.

4 A climate of peace enables the process of healing to begin. It transforms the prospects for political progress, building on that already made in the Talks process. Everyone now has a role to play in moving irreversibly beyond the failures of the past and creating new relationships capable of perpetuating peace with freedom and justice.

5 In the Joint Declaration both Governments set themselves the aim of fostering agreement and reconciliation, leading to a new political framework founded on consent. A vital dimension of this three-stranded process is the search, through dialogue with the relevant Northern Ireland parties, for new institutions and structures to take account of the totality of relationships and to enable the people of Ireland to work together in all areas of common interest while fully respecting their diversity.

6 Both Governments are conscious of the widespread desire, throughout both islands and more widely, to see negotiations underway as soon as possible. They also acknowledge the many requests, from parties in Northern Ireland and elsewhere, for both Governments to set out their views on how agreement might be reached on relationships within the island of Ireland and between the peoples of these islands.

7 In this Framework Document both Governments therefore describe a shared understanding reached between them on the parameters of a possible outcome to the Talks process, consistent with the Joint Declaration and the statement of 26 March 1991. Through this they hope to give impetus and direction to the process and to show that a fair and honourable accommodation can be envisaged across all the relationships, which would enable people to work constructively for their mutual benefit, without compromising the essential principles or the long-term aspirations or interests of either tradition or of either community.

8 Both Governments are aware that the approach in this document presents challenges to strongly-held positions on all sides. However, a new beginning in relationships means addressing fundamental issues in a new way and inevitably requires significant movement from all sides. This document is not a rigid blueprint to be imposed but both Governments believe it sets out a realistic and balanced framework for agreement which could be achieved, with flexibility and goodwill on all sides, in comprehensive negotiations with the relevant political parties in Northern Ireland. In this spirit, both Governments offer this document for consideration and accordingly strongly commend it to the parties, the people in the island of Ireland and more widely.

9 The primary objective of both Governments in their approach to Northern Ireland is to promote and establish agreement among the people of the island of Ireland, building on the Joint Declaration. To this end they will both deploy their political resources with the aim of securing a new and comprehensive agreement involving the relevant political parties in Northern Ireland and commanding the widest possible support.

10 They take as guiding principles for their co-operation in search of this agreement:

- (i) the principle of self-determination, as set out in the Joint Declaration;
- (ii) that the consent of the governed is an essential ingredient for stability in any political arrangement;
- (iii) that agreement must be pursued and established by exclusively democratic, peaceful means, without resort to violence or coercion;
- (iv) that any new political arrangements must be based on full respect for, and protection and expression of, the rights

and identities of both traditions in Ireland and even-handedly afford both communities in Northern Ireland parity of esteem and treatment, including equality of opportunity and advantage.

11 They acknowledge that in Northern Ireland, unlike the situation which prevails elsewhere throughout both islands, there is a fundamental absence of consensus about constitutional issues. There are deep divisions between the members of the two main traditions living there over their respective senses of identity and allegiance, their views on the present status of Northern Ireland and their vision of future relationships in Ireland and between the two islands. However, the two Governments also recognise that the large majority of people, in both parts of Ireland, are at one in their commitment to the democratic process and in their desire to resolve political differences by peaceful means.

12 In their search for political agreement, based on consent, the two Governments are determined to address in a fresh way all of the relationships involved. Their aim is to overcome the legacy of division by reconciling the rights of both traditions in the fullest and most equitable manner. They will continue to work towards and encourage the achievement of agreement, so as to realise the goal set out in the statement of 26 March 1991 of "a new beginning for relationships within Northern Ireland, within the island of Ireland and between the peoples of these islands".

13 The two Governments will work together with the parties to achieve a comprehensive accommodation, the implementation of which would include interlocking and mutually supportive institutions across the three strands, including:

(a) structures within Northern Ireland (paragraphs 22 and 23)—to enable elected representatives in Northern Ireland to exercise shared administrative and legislative control over all those matters that can be agreed across both communities and which can most effectively and appropriately be dealt with at that level;

(b) North/South institutions (paragraphs 24–38)—with clear identity and purpose, to enable representatives of democratic institutions, North and South, to enter into new, co-operative and constructive relationships; to promote agreement among the people of the island of Ireland; to carry out on a democratically accountable basis delegated executive, harmonising and consultative functions over a range of designated matters to be agreed; and to serve to acknowledge and reconcile the rights, identities and aspirations of the two major traditions;

(c) East–West structures (paragraphs 39–49)—to enhance the existing basis for co-operation between the two Governments, and to promote, support and underwrite the fair and effective operation of the new arrangements.

Constitutional Issues

14 Both Governments accept that agreement on an overall settlement requires, inter alia, a balanced accommodation of the differing views of the two main traditions on the constitutional issues in relation to the special position of Northern Ireland.

15 Given the absence of consensus and depth of divisions between the two main traditions in Northern Ireland, the two Governments agree that such an accommodation will involve an agreed new approach to the traditional constitutional doctrines on both sides. This would be aimed at enhancing and codifying the fullest attainable measure of consent across both traditions in Ireland and fostering the growth of consensus between them.

16 In their approach to Northern Ireland they will apply the principle of self-determination by the people of Ireland on the basis set out in the Joint Declaration: the British Government recognise that it is for the people of Ireland alone, by agreement between the two parts respectively and without external impediment, to exercise their right of self-determination on the basis of consent, freely and concurrently given, North and South, to bring about a united Ireland, if that is their wish; the Irish Government accept that the democratic right of self-determination by the people of Ireland as a whole must be achieved and exercised with and subject to the agreement and consent of a majority of the people of Northern Ireland.

17 New arrangements should be in accordance with the commitments in the Anglo-Irish Agreement and in the Joint Declaration. They should acknowledge that it would be wrong to make any change in the status of Northern Ireland save with the consent of a majority of the people of Northern Ireland. If in future a majority of the people there wish for and formally consent to the establishment of a united Ireland, the two Governments will introduce and support legislation to give effect to that wish.

18 Both Governments recognise that Northern Ireland's current constitutional status reflects and relies upon the present wish of a majority of its people. They also acknowledge that at present a substantial minority of its people wish for a united Ireland. Reaffirming the commitment to encourage, facilitate and enable the achievement of agreement over a period among all the people who inhabit the island, they acknowledge that the option of a sovereign united Ireland does not command the consent of the unionist tradition, nor does the existing status of Northern Ireland command the consent of the nationalist tradition. Against this background, they acknowledge the need for new arrangements and structures—to reflect the reality of diverse aspirations, to reconcile as fully as possible the rights of both traditions, and to promote co-operation between them, so as to foster the process of developing agreement and consensus between all the people of Ireland.

19 They agree that future arrangements relating to Northern Ireland, and Northern Ireland's wider relationships, should respect the full and equal legitimacy and worth of the identity, sense of allegiance, aspiration and ethos of both the unionist and nationalist communities there. Consequently, both Governments commit themselves to the principle that institutions and arrangements in Northern Ireland and North/South institutions should afford both communities secure and satisfactory political, administrative and symbolic expression and protection. In particular, they commit themselves to entrenched provisions guaranteeing equitable and effective political participation for whichever community finds itself in a minority position by reference to the Northern Ireland framework, or the wider Irish framework, as the case may be, consequent upon the operation of the principle of consent.

20 The British Government reaffirm that they will uphold the democratic wish of a greater number of the people of Northern Ireland on the issue of whether they prefer to support the Union or a sovereign united Ireland. On this basis, they reiterate that they have no selfish strategic or economic interest in Northern Ireland. For as long as the democratic wish of the people of Northern Ireland is for no change in its present status, the British Government pledge that their jurisdiction there will be exercised with rigorous impartiality on behalf of all the people of Northern Ireland in their diversity. It will be founded on the principles outlined in the previous paragraph with emphasis on full respect for, and equality of, civil, political, social and cultural rights and freedom from discrimination for all citizens, on parity of esteem, and on just and equal treatment for the identity, ethos and aspirations of both communities. The British Government will discharge their responsibilities in a way which does not prejudice the freedom of the people of Northern Ireland to determine, by peaceful and democratic means, its future constitutional status, whether in remaining a part of the United Kingdom or in forming part of a united Ireland. They will be equally cognizant of either option and open to its democratic realisation, and will not impede the latter option, their primary interest being to see peace, stability and reconciliation established by agreement among the people who inhabit the island. This new approach for Northern Ireland, based on the continuing willingness to accept the will of a majority of the people there, will be enshrined in British constitutional legislation embodying the principles and commitments in the Joint Declaration and this Framework Document, either by amendment of the Government of Ireland Act 1920 or by its replacement by appropriate new legislation, and appropriate new provisions entrenched by Agreement.

21 As part of an agreement confirming the foregoing understanding between the two Governments on constitutional issues, the Irish Government will introduce and support proposals for change in the Irish Constitution to implement the commitments in the Joint

Declaration. These changes in the Irish Constitution will fully reflect the principle of consent in Northern Ireland and demonstrably be such that no territorial claim of right to jurisdiction over Northern Ireland contrary to the will of a majority of its people is asserted, while maintaining the existing birthright of everyone born in either jurisdiction in Ireland to be part, as of right, of the Irish nation. They will enable a new Agreement to be ratified which will include, as part of a new and equitable dispensation for Northern Ireland embodying the principles and commitments in the Joint Declaration and this Framework Document, recognition by both Governments of the legitimacy of whatever choice is freely exercised by a majority of the people of Northern Ireland with regard to its constitutional status, whether they prefer to continue to support the Union or a sovereign united Ireland.

Structures in Northern Ireland

22 Both Governments recognise that new political structures within Northern Ireland must depend on the co-operation of elected representatives there. They confirm that cross-community agreement is an essential requirement for the establishment and operation of such structures. They strongly favour and will support provision for cross-community consensus in relation to decisions affecting the basic rights, concerns and fundamental interests of both communities, for example on the lines adumbrated in Strand 1 discussions in the 1992 round-table talks.

23 While the principles and overall context for such new structures are a recognised concern of both Governments in the exercise of their respective responsibilities, they consider that the structures themselves would be most effectively negotiated as part of a comprehensive three-stranded process, in direct dialogue involving the relevant political parties in Northern Ireland who would be called upon to operate them.

North/South Institutions

24 Both Governments consider that new institutions should be created to cater adequately for present and future political, social and economic inter-connections on the island of Ireland, enabling representatives of the main traditions, North and South, to enter agreed dynamic, new, co-operative and constructive relationships.

25 Both Governments agree that these institutions should include a North/South body involving Heads of Department on both sides and duly established and maintained by legislation in both sovereign Parliaments. This body would bring together these Heads of Department representing the Irish Government and new democratic institutions in Northern Ireland, to discharge or oversee delegated executive, harmonising or consultative functions, as appropriate, over a range of matters which the two Governments designate in the first instance in agreement with the

parties or which the two administrations, North and South, subsequently agree to designate. It is envisaged that, in determining functions to be discharged or overseen by the North/South body, whether by executive action, harmonisation or consultation, account will be taken of:

(i) the common interest in a given matter on the part of both parts of the island; or
(ii) the mutual advantage of addressing a matter together; or
(iii) the mutual benefit which may derive from it being administered by the North/South body; or
(iv) the achievement of economies of scale and the avoidance of unnecessary duplication of effort.

In relevant posts in each of the two administrations participation in the North/South body would be a duty of service. Both Governments believe that the legislation should provide for a clear institutional identity and purpose for the North/South body. It would also establish the body's terms of reference, legal status and arrangements for political, legal, administrative and financial accountability. The North/South body could operate through, or oversee, a range of functionally-related subsidiary bodies or other entities established to administer designated functions on an all-island or cross-border basis.

26 Specific arrangements would need to be developed to apply to EU matters. Any EU matter relevant to the competence of either administration could be raised for consideration in the North/South body. Across all designated matters and in accordance with the delegated functions, both Governments agree that the body will have an important role, with their support and co-operation and in consultation with them, in developing on a continuing basis an agreed approach for the whole island in respect of the challenges and opportunities of the European Union. In respect of matters designated at the executive level, which would include all EC programmes and initiatives to be implemented on a cross-border or island-wide basis in Ireland, the body itself would be responsible, subject to the Treaty obligations of each Government, for the implementation and management of EC policies and programmes on a joint basis. This would include the preparation, in consultation with the two Governments, of joint submissions under EC programmes and initiatives and their joint monitoring and implementation, although individual projects could be implemented either jointly or separately.

27 Both Governments envisage regular and frequent meetings of the North/South body:

(i) to discharge the functions agreed for it in relation to a range of matters designated for treatment on an all-Ireland or cross-border basis;
(ii) to oversee the work of subsidiary bodies.

28 The two Governments envisage that legislation in the sovereign Parliaments should designate those functions which should, from the outset, be discharged or overseen by the North/South body; and they will seek agreement on these, as on other features of North/South arrangements, in discussion with the relevant political parties in Northern Ireland. It would also be open to the North/South body to recommend to the respective administrations and legislatures for their consideration that new functions should be designated to be discharged or overseen by that body; and to recommend that matters already designated should be moved on the scale between consultation, harmonisation and executive action. Within those responsibilities transferred to new institutions in Northern Ireland, the British Government have no limits of their own to impose on the nature and extent of functions which could be agreed for designation at the outset or, subsequently, between the Irish Government and the Northern Ireland administration. Both Governments expect that significant responsibilities, including meaningful functions at executive level, will be a feature of such agreement. The British Government believe that, in principle, any function devolved to the institutions in Northern Ireland could be so designated, subject to any necessary savings in respect of the British Government's powers and duties, for example to ensure compliance with EU and international obligations. The Irish Government also expect to designate a comparable range of functions.

29 Although both Governments envisage that representatives of North and South in the body could raise for discussion any matter of interest to either side which falls within the competence of either administration, it is envisaged, as already mentioned, that its designated functions would fall into three broad categories:

consultative: the North/South body would be a forum where the two sides would consult on any aspect of designated matters on which either side wished to hold consultations. Both sides would share a duty to exchange information and to consult about existing and future policy, though there would be no formal requirement that agreement would be reached or that policy would be harmonised or implemented jointly, but the development of mutual understanding or common or agreed positions would be the general goal;

harmonising: in respect of these designated responsibilities there would be, in addition to the duty to exchange information and to consult on the formulation of policy, an obligation on both sides to use their best endeavours to reach agreement on a common policy and to make determined efforts to overcome any obstacles in the way of that objective, even though its implementation might be undertaken by the two administrations separately;

executive: in the case of these designated responsibilities the North/South body would itself be directly responsible for the establishment of an agreed policy and for its implementation on a joint basis. It would however be open to the body, where appropriate, to agree that the implementation of the agreed policy would be undertaken either by existing bodies, acting in an agency capacity, whether jointly or separately, North and South, or by new bodies specifically created and mandated for this purpose.

30 In this light, both Governments are continuing to give consideration to the range of functions that might, with the agreement of the parties, be designated at the outset and accordingly they will be ready to make proposals in that regard in future discussions with the relevant Northern Ireland parties.

31 By way of illustration, it is intended that these proposals would include at the executive level a range of functions, clearly defined in scope, from within the following broad categories:

sectors involving a natural or physical all-Ireland framework;
EC programmes and initiatives;
marketing and promotion activities abroad;
culture and heritage.

32 Again, by way of illustration, the Governments would make proposals at the harmonising level for a broader range of functions, clearly defined in scope (including, as appropriate, relevant EU aspects), from within the following categories:

Aspects of

agriculture and fisheries
industrial development
consumer affairs
transport
energy
trade
health
social welfare
education and
economic policy.

33 By way of example, the category of agriculture and fisheries might include agricultural and fisheries research, training and advisory services, and animal welfare; health might include co-operative ventures in medical, paramedical and nursing training, cross-border provision of hospital services and major emergency/accident planning; and education might include mutual recognition of teacher qualifications, co-operative ventures in higher education, in teacher training, in education for mutual understanding and in education for specialised needs.

34 The Governments also expect that a wide range of functions would be designated at the consultative level.

35 Both Governments envisage that all decisions within the body would be by agreement between the two sides. The Heads of Department on each side would operate within the overall terms of reference mandated by legislation in the two sovereign Parliaments. They would exercise their powers in accordance with the rules for democratic authority and accountability for this function in force in the Oireachtas and in new institutions in Northern Ireland. The operation of the North/South body's functions would be subject to regular scrutiny in agreed political institutions in Northern Ireland and the Oireachtas respectively.

36 Both Governments expect that there would be a Parliamentary Forum, with representatives from agreed political institutions in Northern Ireland and members of the Oireachtas, to consider a wide range of matters of mutual interest.

37 Both Governments envisage that the framework would include administrative support staffed jointly by members of the Northern Ireland Civil Service and the Irish Civil Service. They also envisage that both administrations will need to arrange finance for the North/South body and its agencies on the basis that these constitute a necessary public function.

38 Both Governments envisage that this new framework should serve to help heal the divisions among the communities on the island of Ireland; provide a forum for acknowledging the respective identities and requirements of the two major traditions; express and enlarge the mutual acceptance of the validity of those traditions; and promote understanding and agreement among the people and institutions in both parts of the island. The remit of the body should be dynamic, enabling progressive extension by agreement of its functions to new areas. Its role should develop to keep pace with the growth of harmonisation and with greater integration between the two economies.

East–West Structures

39 Both Governments envisage a new and more broadly-based Agreement, developing and extending their co-operation, reflecting the totality of relationships between the two islands, and dedicated to fostering co-operation, reconciliation and agreement in Ireland at all levels.

40 They intend that under such a new Agreement a standing Intergovernmental Conference will be maintained, chaired by the designated Irish Minister and by the Secretary of State for Northern Ireland. It would be supported by a Permanent Secretariat of civil servants from both Governments.

41 The Conference will be a forum through which the two Governments will work together in pursuance of their joint objectives of securing agreement and reconciliation amongst the people of

the island of Ireland and of laying the foundations for a peaceful and harmonious future based on mutual trust and understanding between them.

42 The Conference will provide a continuing institutional expression for the Irish Government's recognised concern and role in relation to Northern Ireland. The Irish Government will put forward views and proposals on issues falling within the ambit of the new Conference or involving both Governments, and determined efforts will be made to resolve any differences between the two Governments. The Conference will be the principal instrument for an intensification of the co-operation and partnership between both Governments, with particular reference to the principles contained in the Joint Declaration, in this Framework Document and in the new Agreement, on a wide range of issues concerned with Northern Ireland and with the relations between the two parts of the island of Ireland. It will facilitate the promotion of lasting peace, stability, justice and reconciliation among the people of the island of Ireland and maintenance of effective security co-operation between the two Governments.

43 Both Governments believe that there should also be provision in the Agreement for developing co-operation between the two Governments and both islands on a range of "East–West" issues and bilateral matters of mutual interest not covered by other specific arrangements, either through the Anglo-Irish Intergovernmental Council, the Conference or otherwise.

44 Both Governments accept that issues of law and order in Northern Ireland are closely intertwined with the issues of political consensus. For so long as these matters are not devolved, it will be for the Government to consider ways in which a climate of peace, new institutions and the growth of political agreement may offer new possibilities and opportunities for enhancing community identification with policing in Northern Ireland, while maintaining the most effective possible deployment of the resources of each Government in their common determination to combat crime and prevent any possible recourse to the use or threat of violence for political ends, from any source whatsoever.

45 The Governments envisage that matters for which responsibility is transferred to new political institutions in Northern Ireland will be excluded from consideration in the Conference, except to the extent that the continuing responsibilities of the Secretary of State for Northern Ireland are relevant, or that cross-border aspects of transferred issues are not otherwise provided for, or in the circumstances described in the following paragraph.

46 The Intergovernmental Conference will be a forum for the two Governments jointly to keep under review the workings of the Agreement and to promote, support and underwrite the fair and effective operation of all its provisions and the new arrangements

established under it. Where either Government considers that any institution, established as part of the overall accommodation, is not properly functioning within the Agreement or that a breach of the Agreement has otherwise occurred, the Conference shall consider the matter on the basis of a shared commitment to arrive at a common position or, where that is not possible, to agree a procedure to resolve the difference between them. If the two Governments conclude that a breach has occurred in any of the above circumstances, either Government may make proposals for remedy and adequate measures to redress the situation shall be taken. However, each Government will be responsible for the implementation of such measures of redress within its own jurisdiction. There would be no derogation from the sovereignty of either Government; each will retain responsibility for the decisions and administration of government within its own jurisdiction.

47 In the event that devolved institutions in Northern Ireland ceased to operate, and direct rule from Westminster was reintroduced, the British Government agree that other arrangements would be made to implement the commitment to promote co-operation at all levels between the people, North and South, representing both traditions in Ireland, as agreed by the two Governments in the Joint Declaration, and to ensure that the co-operation that had been developed through the North/South body be maintained.

48 Both Governments envisage that representatives of agreed political institutions in Northern Ireland may be formally associated with the work of the Conference, in a manner and to an extent to be agreed by both Governments after consultation with them. This might involve giving them advance notice of what is to be discussed in the Conference, enabling them to express views to either Government and inviting them to participate in various aspects of the work of the Conference. Other more structured arrangements could be devised by agreement.

49 The Conference will also be a framework for consultation and co-ordination between both Governments and the new North/South institutions, where the wider role of the two Governments is particularly relevant to the work of those institutions, for example in a co-ordinated approach on EU issues. It would be for consideration by both Governments, in consultation with the relevant parties in the North, or with the institutions after they have been established, whether to achieve this through formal or ad hoc arrangements.

Protection of Rights

50 There is a large body of support, transcending the political divide, for the comprehensive protection and guarantee of fundamental human rights. Acknowledging this, both Governments envisage

that the arrangements set out in this Framework Document will be complemented and underpinned by an explicit undertaking in the Agreement on the part of each Government, equally, to ensure in its jurisdiction in the island of Ireland, in accordance with its constitutional arrangements, the systematic and effective protection of common specified civil, political, social and cultural rights. They will discuss and seek agreement with the relevant political parties in Northern Ireland as to what rights should be so specified and how they might best be further protected, having regard to each Government's overall responsibilities including its international obligations. Each Government will introduce appropriate legislation in its jurisdiction to give effect to any such measure of agreement.

51 In addition, both Governments would encourage democratic representatives from both jurisdictions in Ireland to adopt a Charter or Covenant, which might reflect and endorse agreed measures for the protection of the fundamental rights of everyone living in Ireland. It could also pledge a commitment to mutual respect and to the civil rights and religious liberties of both communities, including:

the right of free political thought;

the right to freedom and expression of religion;

the right to pursue democratically national and political aspirations;

the right to seek constitutional change by peaceful and legitimate means;

the right to live wherever one chooses without hindrance; and

the right to equal opportunity in all social and economic activity, regardless of class, creed, gender or colour.

52 This Charter or Covenant might also contain a commitment to the principle of consent in the relationships between the two traditions in Ireland. It could incorporate also an enduring commitment on behalf of all the people of the island to guarantee and protect the rights, interests, ethos and dignity of the unionist community in any all-Ireland framework that might be developed with consent in the future, to at least the same extent as provided for the nationalist community in the context of Northern Ireland under the structures and provisions of the new Agreement.

53 The Covenant might also affirm on behalf of all traditions in Ireland a solemn commitment to the exclusively peaceful resolution of all differences between them including in relation to all issues of self-determination, and a solemn repudiation of all recourse to violence between them for any political end or purpose.

Conclusion

54 Both Governments agree that the issues set out in this Framework Document should be examined in the most comprehensive

attainable negotiations with democratically mandated political parties in Northern Ireland which abide exclusively by peaceful means and wish to join in dialogue on the way ahead.

55 Both Governments intend that the outcome of these negotiations will be submitted for democratic ratification through referendums, North and South.

56 Both Governments believe that the present climate of peace, which owes much to the imagination, courage and steadfastness of all those who have suffered from violence, offers the best prospect for the Governments and the parties in Northern Ireland to work to secure agreement and consent to a new political accommodation. To accomplish that would be an inestimable prize for all, and especially for people living in Northern Ireland, who have so much to gain from such an accommodation, in which the divisions of the past are laid aside for ever and differences are resolved by exclusively political means. Both Governments believe that a new political dispensation, such as they set out in this Framework Document, achieved through agreement and reconciliation and founded on the principle of consent, would achieve that objective and transform relationships in Northern Ireland, in the island of Ireland and between both islands.

57 With agreement, co-operation to the mutual benefit of all living in Ireland could develop without impediment, attaining its full potential for stimulating economic growth and prosperity. New arrangements could return power, authority and responsibility to locally-elected representatives in Northern Ireland on a basis acceptable to both sides of the community, enabling them to work together for the common welfare and interests of all the community. The diversity of identities and allegiances could be regarded by all as a source of mutual enrichment, rather than a threat to either side. The divisive issue of sovereignty might cease to be symbolic of the domination of one community over another. It would instead be for decision under agreed ground-rules, fair and balanced towards both aspirations, through a process of democratic persuasion governed by the principle of consent rather than by threat, fear or coercion. In such circumstances the Governments hope that the relationship between the traditions in Northern Ireland could become a positive bond of further understanding, co-operation and amity, rather than a source of contention, between the wider British and Irish democracies.

58 Accordingly, the British and Irish Governments offer for consideration and strongly commend these proposals, trusting that, with generosity and goodwill, the peoples of these islands will build on them a new and lasting agreement.

Glossary

Anglo-Irish Agreement A document agreed to by the Fine Gael/Labour coalition government of Ireland and Mrs. Thatcher's Conservative government in the United Kingdom in 1985. It stipulates that there shall be no change in the constitutional position of Northern Ireland for so long as the majority wishes to remain as part of the United Kingdom.

Articles Two and Three of the Irish Constitution These two provisions of the Irish Constitution, dating from 1937, lay claim to all thirty-two counties of Ireland, and are often cited by Unionists of the Six Counties as the major hurdle to their co-operation with the Dublin government in any talks concerning the future of the Six Counties.

B-Specials A Protestant state militia first formed in 1920 by the Unionist government from former UVF and British army members in the Six Counties as a back-up force for the police in helping maintain Protestant ascendancy. After the "troubles" broke out in late 1969, their activities so outraged British Prime Minister Harold Wilson that they were disbanded and reconstituted as the Ulster Defence Regiment (UDR) in 1970.

Bloody Sunday January 30, 1972. Thirteen people attending a demonstration in Derry against internment were killed by British soldiers.

CAP Common Agricultural Policy agreed among EU states.

Clann na Gael An Irish-American Nationalist organisation founded in 1867 in the wake of the failed Fenian rising and later linked with the IRB. Its activities included fund-raising, the heightening of awareness and the raising of support for Irish independence. It was the Clann under John Devoy that helped to fund the 1916 Rising.

Conservative Party One of Britain's two main political parties, the Conservatives are associated with right-of-centre politics. They are allied with the Unionist parties in Northern Ireland.

Dáil Éireann Irish Parliament.

Downing Street Declaration A statement issued in December 1993 by the British and Irish governments granting the right of self-determination to bring about a United Ireland if that is the wish of North and South.

DUP Democratic Unionist Party, led by Revd. Ian Paisley.

EEC European Economic Community. Founded in 1957, this economic union now has sixteen member states. Ireland joined in 1973. Now entitled European Union (EU).

Fianna Fáil "Warriors of Destiny". Founded in 1926 by Éamon de Valera after split with Sinn Féin, it is the largest and most powerful of the Irish political parties.

Fine Gael The second largest political party in the Irish Republic, formed in 1933 from the National Centre Party, the Blueshirts and Cumann na nGaedhael.

Friends of Ireland An influential group of US politicians and businessmen with a strong interest in Irish affairs. Originally made up of Speakers Thomas P. O'Neill and Thomas Foley, and Senators Edward M. Kennedy, Daniel Moynihan and Christopher Dodd.

GATT General Agreement on Tariffs and Trade. Economic policy agreed almost worldwide.

H-Block hunger-strikes In 1981, ten republican prisoners including Bobby Sands died on hunger strike in the Maze Prison seeking the status of political prisoners.

Home Rule A term first used in the 1860s, it meant an Irish legislature with responsibility for domestic affairs. At first much sought after by Irish patriots including Parnell, it became an inadequate aspiration for nationalists. The idea was rejected utterly by Unionists, who feared it might lead to what they called "Rome Rule" i.e too much power in the hands of Roman Catholics.

INLA Irish National Liberation Army. An IRA splinter group.

Internment The holding of suspected terrorists without trial in Northern Ireland. Used in 1922, 1939, 1956 and 1971–5, internment has only been used against Republicans, never against Unionist extremists.

IRA Irish Republican Army.

IRB Irish Republican Brotherhood, the Fenians, set up in 1858 as a revolutionary movement. It recognised itself as the provisional governing body of a free and independent Ireland. Re-organised by Michael Collins after the failed Easter Rising, it in effect became the leadership cadre of the Volunteers (IRA).

IRSP Irish Republican Socialist Party. Political wing of the INLA.

Labour Party (Irish Republic) The third largest political party in the Republic of Ireland.

Labour Party (UK) One of Britain's two main political parties. It is associated with the labour unions and left-of-centre politics.

Loyalists Loyal to the Union, these are Ulster Protestants opposed to a thirty-two county Ireland. (Same as Unionists.)

Maastricht Treaty An agreement reached by the members of the EU in Maastricht, Netherlands, in 1992, which lays out several important further steps in the transformation of the Union into a closer federation, and gives new powers to the European Parliament and government organisations.

Marching Season See Twelfth of July.

NICRA Northern Ireland Civil Rights Association. Established in February 1967, it spearheaded the early years of the civil rights campaign.

NORAID North American Aid. An American organisation that raises money for Irish Republican causes.

Official Irish Republican Army In 1970 the IRA split into the Official IRA and the Provisional IRA, which became the dominant grouping. The OIRA maintained the old line of the IRA, the wish for a socialist thirty-two county Ireland.

Orange Order (Orangemen) Name taken from the victory of Protestant William of Orange over Catholic King James II. A powerful sectarian order of Protestants. No Catholic and no-one whose close relatives are Catholic may be a member. It played an important part in defeating Home Rule.

Provisionals (Provos) Now the major IRA force.

Republicans Supporting a thirty-two county Republic of Ireland.

RUC Royal Ulster Constabulary. Police force in the Six Counties.

SAS Special Air Services. The special operations force of the British Army against whom most allegations of carrying out a shoot-to-kill policy are directed by Nationalists.

SDLP Social Democratic and Labour Party. Constitutional Nationalist party of the Six Counties, founded in 1970 believing in the necessity of majority consent for a united Ireland.

Seanad Translates as "Senate". Upper house of Parliament (the Dáil) in Ireland.

Sinn Féin "Ourselves Alone". Political party and wing of the Provisional IRA.

Six Counties Six of the nine counties which make up the province of Ulster. The Six Counties have been part of the United Kingdom since the Government of Ireland Act of 1920.

Stormont Seat of the Northern Irish Parliament from 1932 to 1972 when direct rule from Westminster was re-established.

Sunningdale Agreement Signed in December 1973, between the British Conservative Government of Edward Heath and the Irish Government led by Liam Cosgrave, it established a power-sharing government and Council of Ireland. It lasted five months.

Tánaiste Deputy Prime Minister of the Republic of Ireland.

Taoiseach Prime Minister of the Republic of Ireland.

Thirty-Two Counties The Republic of Ireland and the Six Counties—a united Ireland.

Twelfth of July Commemoration of the Battle of the Boyne every year by the Orange Order, the "marching season". More than parades and pageants, this is a time when Unionist fervour is at its height and clashes occur regularly with Catholics.

Twenty-Six Counties The Republic of Ireland.

UDA Ulster Defence Association. The major Protestant paramilitary group. UDA spokesmen have advocated that Ulster be independent of both Britain and Ireland. Now outlawed, it is alleged to have links with the DUP and UDR.

UDR Ulster Defence Regiment. Formed in 1970 to replace the old B-Special Corps. It too was heavily criticised and was placed under British Army control in 1992.

UFF Ulster Freedom Fighters. A UDA group which has claimed responsibility for several sectarian murders.

Ulster This should correspond to the the ancient nine-county Irish province of Ulster. However, when the State was being set up, the Unionists rejected the nine-county unit because it contained too many Catholics, and settled for the six counties which they could control. The term is now commonly, but erroneously, used by Unionists to refer to the Six Counties.

Unionists Those supporting the 1800 Act of Union when Ireland became part of the United Kingdom and totally opposed to any breaking of ties of the Six Counties with Britain. (Same as Loyalists.)

UVF Ulster Volunteer Force founded in 1912 as a private army to resist Home Rule and armed with 25,000 German rifles. Many members of the UVF enlisted in the British army and served in a separate unit, the 36th (Ulster Division). In the late 1920s, the UVF was involved in pogroms and other attacks on Catholics. The name was revived in 1966 by a loyalist sectarian paramilitary group which murdered two Catholics in that year and later planted the bombs that led to the fall of O'Neill. It remains in existence as a loyalist paramilitary organisation.

Glossary of Names

Adams, Gerry Leader of Sinn Féin 1983– . Prepared basis for present Irish Peace Initiative in talks with John Hume.

Atkins, Humphrey Secretary of State for N. Ireland 1979–81.

Brooke, Peter Secretary of State for Northern Ireland 1989–92.

Bruton, John Leader of Fine Gael 1990– . Taoiseach 1994–

Burke, Edmund (1729–97) A politician and essayist, he opposed the French Revolution of 1789 and sought to win over Irish Catholics by granting them concessions.

Callaghan, James British Home Secretary 1967–70 and Labour Prime Minister 1976–79.

Churchill, Winston (1874–1965) British Conservative Prime Minister during World War II.

Collins, Michael (1890–1922) Member of the Volunteers in the 1916 Rising, Minister of Home Affairs and later Minister of Finance in the First Dáil, and director of organisation and intelligence for the IRA. One of the signatories of the Anglo-Irish Treaty of 1921 and subsequently the first Provisional President and Commander-in-Chief of the government forces in the Civil War. Killed in an ambush in 1922.

Cooper, Ivan Co-founding member of SDLP.

Craig, William Minister of Home Affairs in Northern Ireland 1963–4, Minister of Health and Local Government 1964, Minister of Development 1965, and Minister of Home Affairs again in 1966–8. Established the Ulster Vanguard Party in 1972 with strong support from paramilitaries.

Currie, Austin Previously Nationalist Party MP in Northern Ireland. In 1968, he protested strongly against unfair housing allocation. He later moved to the Republic of Ireland and joined Fine Gael.

De Valera, Éamon (1882–1975) Commandant in the Irish Volunteers in the 1916 Rising, he was sentenced to death but was reprieved, becoming President of Sinn Féin in 1917 and President of the Dáil in 1919. Toured America fundraising between

June 1919 and January 1921. Opposed the Treaty and was the political leader of the anti-Treaty forces in the Civil War of 1922–3. Founded Fianna Fáil in 1926 and was Taoiseach 1932–48, 1951–4, 1957–9 and President of the Republic 1959–73.

Devlin, Patrick Co-founder of the SDLP. Left the party in 1977.

Devoy, John (1842–1928) Joined the Fenians, became an organiser for the IRB. Imprisoned for five years, then sent in exile to the US where he became editor of *The Gaelic-American* and collected funds for the Irish Volunteers.

Faulkner, Brian (1921–77) Unionist MP for East Down at Stormont 1949–73, Minister of Home Affairs 1959–63, Minister of Commerce 1963–9, Minister of Development 1969–71, Prime Minister 1971–2. Set up breakaway Unionist Party of Northern Ireland in 1974. Chief Executive of Northern Ireland Executive in 1974. Died in a horse-riding accident.

Fitt, Gerry Co-founding member and leader 1970–79 of SDLP.

FitzGerald, Garret Leader of Fine Gael 1977–87. Taoiseach 1981–2, and 1982–7.

Gladstone, William Ewart (1809–98) British Labour Prime Minister 1868–74, 1880–85, and 1892–4. Secured disestablishment of Church of Ireland in 1869. Introduced the first of a series of Land Acts in 1870. Negotiated with Parnell. His first Home Rule Bill was defeated in 1886, his second was lost in the House of Lords in 1893.

Goldsmith, Oliver (1730–74) Dramatist. His play *She Stoops to Conquer* was first performed at Covent Garden, London, in 1773.

Grattan, Henry (1746–1820) Demanded in House of Commons that Ireland should have legislative independence, though insisting that Ireland remain linked to the British Crown. The parliament that was subsequently established in Dublin in 1783 was known as Grattan's Parliament. Its last session took place in 1799.

Haughey, Charles Leader of Fianna Fáil 1979–92. Taoiseach 1979–81, 1982, 1987–89, and 1989–92.

Heath, Edward British Conservative Prime Minister 1970–74. Signed Sunningdale Agreement of 1973.

Mayhew, Patrick Secretary of State for Northern Ireland 1992– .

McAteer, Edward Leader of Nationalist Party in opposition in Stormont 1965–9 when he lost his seat to John Hume.

MacSwiney, Terence (1879–1920) Author of plays, poetry and political journalism and of *Principals of Freedom*, and full-time organiser of the Irish Volunteers. Elected to first Dáil for West Cork, and then Lord Mayor of Cork. He was arrested in Cork City Hall in 1920 and his subsequent hunger strike focused world attention on Ireland. He died on the seventy-fourth day of his hunger strike in Brixton Prison.

Major, John British Conservative Prime Minister 1990– . Signed 1993 Downing Street Declaration.

O'Connell, Daniel (1775–1847) Co-founder of the Catholic Association in 1823 which brought about Catholic emancipation in 1829. A lawyer, he believed in achieving reform solely through peaceful and political means. Worked for reform of land laws. Orated passionately to mass rallies throughout the country. He is known in Ireland as The Liberator.

O'Donnell, Red Hugh (1571–1602) Kidnapped by the English and held in Dublin Castle for four years before managing to escape. After the Battle of Kinsale in 1601, he left Ireland for Spain and died there a year later.

O'Hanlon, Patrick Co-founder of the SDLP.

O'Neill, Hugh (1540–1616) Earl of Tyrone. Marched to Kinsale to meet the Spanish army which came under Don Juan del Aquila to help in the insurrection against the English.

O'Neill, Terence (1914–90) Six County Minister for Finance 1956–63, and Prime Minister of Northern Ireland 1963–9. Visited the Irish Government in Dublin in 1965 and 1967.

Paisley, Ian Loyalist demagogue who, in 1951, set up a "Free Presbyterian Church". From this base he attacked the civil rights campaign, the so-called "Romeward trend" of the Presbyterian Church and the "treachery" of the Unionist leaders who met with many Twenty-Six County politicians. MP for North Antrim since 1970, he founded the Democratic Unionist Party in 1971.

Parnell, Charles Stewart (1846–91) Leader of the Irish Parliamentary Party. Founded the National League to fight for Home Rule. His brilliant political career was cut short by scandal over his affair with Kitty O'Shea, wife of Captain William O'Shea. After her divorce, he married O'Shea but died prematurely in 1891.

Pearse, Pádraig (1879–1916) Teacher, writer and revolutionary, founder of a bilingual school, member of the IRB, he was Commander-in-Chief of the forces of the Irish Republic in the 1916 Rising. One of the signatories of the Proclamation, he was President of the Provisional Government and was executed by the British.

Prior, James Secretary of State for Northern Ireland 1981–4. Published white paper, *Northern Ireland: a framework for devolution.*

Reynolds, Albert Leader of Fianna Fáil and Taoiseach 1992–4. Signed 1993 Downing Street Declaration. Involved in ceasefire negotiations with John Hume and Gerry Adams.

Sands, Bobby (1954–81) Provisional IRA prisoner in the Maze prison. Went on hunger strike in protest against prison regulations. Died after 66 days. Elected as Sinn Féin MP during the strike.

Spring, Dick Leader of Irish Labour Party and Minister for Foreign Affairs. Formed coalition and acted as Tánaiste (deputy Prime Minister) with Fine Gael 1981–2 and 1982–87, with Fianna Fáil 1993–4 and with Fine Gael and Democratic Left 1994– .

Swift, Jonathan (1667–1745) Installed as Dean of St. Patrick's cathedral, Dublin, in 1713. A brilliant essayist and satirist, he wrote the "Drapier Letters" and is most famous for *Gulliver's Travels*, 1726.

Tone, Theobald Wolfe (1763–98) A Protestant barrister, he published *An Argument on Behalf of the Catholics of Ireland.* He urged a reform programme that included Catholic emancipation and believed it could only be achieved if Catholics and Protestants co-operated. He co-founded the Belfast Society of United Irishmen, soon followed by the Dublin Society. Arrested on the French flagship during the 1798 rebellion, he was sentenced to death but committed suicide.

Thatcher, Margaret British Conservative Prime Minister 1979–90.

Whitelaw, William With introduction of direct rule, Secretary of State for Northern Ireland 1972–3. Published green paper, *The Future of Northern Ireland.*

Chronology

12th Century Norman conquest of Ireland, and by English king Henry II.

16th Century Henry VIII declared King of Ireland; split with Pope and establishment of Church of England sets stage for conflict.

1601 The Irish and their Spanish allies defeated by Elizabeth's English force at the Battle of Kinsale, which marked the end of the old Irish world.

1607 "Flight of the Earls" or "Wild Geese". Traumatic exile of leading lords of Ulster.

1608–10 Plantation of confiscated Catholic lands in Ulster by mainly Scottish settlers.

1689 Siege of Derry and defence by the brave outnumbered Protestant loyalists.

1690 Protestant William of Orange defeats Catholic King James II at Oldbridge in the seminal Battle of the Boyne.

1720 Act of Parliament allowing for Westminster to legislate for Ireland.

1783–99 Grattan's Parliament established in Dublin.

1791 The publication of *Argument on Behalf of the Catholics of Ireland* by Protestant Wolfe Tone, seeking Catholic emancipation. Multi-religious Society of United Irishmen founded. Its members strove to change public opinion and argued for electoral and parliamentary reform and swore to obtain Catholic emancipation.

1795 Foundation of the Orange Society (later, Order).

1798 Rising by the United Irishmen, aided by French soldiers. Wolfe Tone arrested and sentenced to death for his part in the organisation of the rebellion; later commits suicide.

1801 Act of Union whereby Ireland becomes part of England.

1823 Catholic Association founded.

1829 Led by Daniel O'Connell, Catholic Emancipation finally achieved. Restrictions on Catholics from taking their place in parliament removed.

1840 Repeal Association founded for the removal of the hated Act of Union.

1842 First issue of *The Nation* by idealistic Young Irelanders.

1845–9 Famine following blight of potato. In this period the population of Ireland is depleted by over two million through starvation, disease or emigration. Beginning of Diaspora.

1848 Young Ireland rising is crushed in its attempts to win self-government for the Irish.

1850 Founding of Irish Tenant League with the aim of achieving fair rent, fixity of tenure and freedom for tenants to sell their holding (the "Three Fs").

1858 The Irish Republican Brotherhood, and the Fenians in the United States, founded by former Young Ireland members. This revolutionary movement's aim was to be independent of Britain, using physical force to achieve this aim.

1869 Disestablishment of the Protestant Church of Ireland.

1873 Home Rule League formed, seeking to achieve control for the Irish over their own local government affairs. Won more than half the Irish seats in the 1874 election.

1875 Protestant landlord Charles Stewart Parnell returned to parliament as a member of the Irish Parliamentary Party.

1876 Clann na Gael, an Irish-American group raising funding and support for Irish independence, joins with IRB.

1879 Irish National Land League founded. Parnell elected president of League whose principal aim was agrarian land reform based on the "Three Fs".

1879–82 The "Land War", violence, protest and the feared "boycott".

1881 Land Act lessening the power of the landlords, in effect the granting of the "Three Fs".

1884 Gaelic Athletic Association (GAA) formed to revive Irish games, harkening to ancient past and glory.

1886 British Prime Minister William Gladstone's Home Rule Bill defeated in the House of Commons by Conservatives.

1890 Split in Irish Party over Parnell's leadership. John Redmond, Joseph Devlin, and John Dillon left with pieces.

1891 Parnell dies.

1892 Ulster Unionist Convention in Belfast, attended by 12,000 unionists opposing Home Rule. First socialist party founded in Ireland, the Belfast Labour Party. National Literary Society formed in Dublin by Yeats and Hyde.

1893 Second Home Rule Bill introduced. Conradh na Gaeilge, the Gaelic League, set up by Dr. Douglas Hyde and Professor Eoin MacNeill, taking its place in the Anglo-Irish literary revival. Primary aim of the league is to restore Irish as the primary spoken language, "hoping to rekindle the dreams of ancient glory".

1896 James Connolly forms Irish Republican Socialist Party.

1900 Cumann na nGaedhael formed by journalist Arthur Griffith.

1905 Republican Dungannon Clubs founded in Belfast.

1906 Arthur Griffith founds and edits the first issue of *Sinn Féin.*

1907 James Larkin leads Dock Strike in Belfast. Sinn Féin League formed from Cumann na nGaedhael and Dungannon Clubs. The league proposes a dual monarchy for Ireland and Britain, declaring the Act of Union to be illegal.

1908 Embryonic Sinn Féin organisation contests its first by-election.

1912 January—Home Rule Bill passed by the House of Commons. September—Over 450,000 people sign the Ulster Covenant to pledge their resistance to the introduction of Home Rule. Edward Carson issues leadership role.

1913 Ulster Volunteer Force set up to protest at Home Rule; arms running from Germany and a provisional government formed in expectation of Home Rule. Great lock-out in Dublin organised by James Larkin and the Irish Transport and General Workers' Union. Citizen Army formed to protect strikers.

1914 Home Rule Act suspended for duration of First World War. Redmond and Irish Party support war.

1916 Easter Rising and Declaration of the Irish Republic by the Provisional Government under Pádraig Pearse and a small group of zealots. Leaders of Rising executed: Pearse, Connolly and others; Éamon de Valera commuted to life imprisonment.

1918 Sinn Féin wins seventy-three of 103 seats in election. Only in Ulster does the old Parliamentary Party keep a foothold with the Unionist members in control.

1919–21 War of Independence (or Black and Tan War) between the Irish Volunteers and the British Army with "Black and Tans" and other Auxiliaries.

1919 Sinn Féin calls first Dáil Éireann in Dublin's Mansion House. Irish Volunteers become known as the IRA, Sinn Féin outlawed.

1920 Government of Ireland Act allowing for two parliaments in Ireland, one in Dublin and one in Belfast.

1921 Anglo-Irish Treaty granting status to Twenty-Six Counties and mandating an oath to the King. Michael Collins and Arthur Griffith become provisional leaders; de Valera opposes with much of IRA.

1922 IRA declared illegal by Northern Irish parliament. Collins shot in skirmish; Griffith dies of natural causes. Saorstát Éireann (Irish Free State) comes into being.

1922–3 Irish Civil War between those accepting and those against the 1921 Treaty.

1925 An agreement between the parliaments of the Irish Free State, Britain and Northern Ireland to keep the border with Northern Ireland.

1927 Fianna Fáil party of de Valera founded in Dublin.

1936 IRA declared illegal in the Irish Free State.

1937 New Constitution of Éire. De Valera comes to power. Articles Two and Three lay claim to the Six Counties. John Hume born in Derry.

1939 IRA begins bombing campaign in England.

1939–45 Éire remains neutral during World War II, the so-called "Emergency".

1949 Éire becomes a republic. UK Act recognises the Republic of Ireland but declares that Northern Ireland will remain part of the UK unless Northern Ireland parliament decides otherwise.

1954 Flags and Emblems Act of Northern Ireland, forbidding the display of flags other than the Union Jack.

1956–62 IRA bombing campaign in Northern Ireland.

1964–8 John Hume made President of the Credit Union League of Ireland.

1965 Hume helps to set up Derry Housing Association.

1966 Ulster Volunteer Force, Protestant paramilitary, outlawed.

1967 Formation of Northern Ireland Civil Rights Association (NICRA).

1968 Marches and demonstrations all over Northern Ireland to protest at injustices by the state against Catholics. Clashes between marchers and police. Four days after being present at riots on 5 October, Hume co-founds and becomes vice-chairman of the Derry Citizens' Action Committee.

1969 Ulster Defence Force (UDF) formed. Hume wins Foyle seat to the Northern Ireland parliament, defeating Nationalist Party candidate Eddie McAteer.

1970 Sinn Féin and IRA split into Official and Provisional IRA. B-Specials disbanded. Social Democratic and Labour Party (SDLP) founded in Northern Ireland under the aegis of Gerry Fitt and John Hume.

1971 Internment (the holding of suspected IRA members without trial) introduced. Democratic Unionist Party formed by Ian Paisley. Northern Ireland Housing Executive set up. Section 31 of Broadcasting Act, 1960, implemented in the Republic.

1972 "Bloody Sunday." Thirteen demonstrators at a banned civil rights march shot dead by British army soldiers in Derry. Fall of Stormont, the Northern Irish parliament. Northern Ireland now ruled directly by Westminster. IRA resume bombing campaign in Britain.

1973 Ireland and UK join EEC. Northern Ireland Assembly set up.

1973–4 Sunningdale attempt at joint Catholic–Protestant rule. Hume appointed as a cabinet minister; collapse of effort.

1974 In Birmingham, six Irish people protesting their innocence were jailed for bombs which killed twenty-one people, and are finally released in 1991.

1975 Ending of internment.

1976 NICRA calls off Rent and Rate strike. Peace People formed in Northern Ireland by Betty Williams and Mairéad Corrigan.

1977 Betty Williams and Mairéad Corrigan awarded Nobel Peace Prize.

1979 In June John Hume is elected to the European Parliament and in November he is elected as leader of SDLP.

1980 Internment law repealed. Republican prisoners start hunger-strike in H-Block in the Maze prison (Long Kesh) as part of protest over right to recognition as political prisoners, and, thus, the right to wear their own clothes.

1981 Ten Republican prisoners die on hunger-strike in the Maze prison, including Bobby Sands MP. Massive unrest and violence. Anglo-Irish Intergovernmental Council established.

1982 IRA explode bombs in Hyde Park and Regent's Park in London, killing 10 people.

1984 The Grand Hotel in Brighton, England, venue for the Conservative Party Conference, is bombed, killing 5 people. Report of the New Ireland Forum published.

1985 Garret FitzGerald and Margaret Thatcher sign Anglo-Irish Agreement, affirming that, as long as the majority in Northern Ireland so wish it, Northern Ireland shall remain part of the United Kingdom.

1987 An IRA bomb in Enniskillen, County Fermanagh, kills 11 people and injures 63 during a war remembrance service. Gordon Wilson's daughter Marie is killed. Subsequently, as senator, he met the IRA to ask them to stop the slaughter.

1988 SAS soldiers shot three unarmed IRA members in Gibraltar. John Hume intensifies economic outreach to the United States. Simultaneous efforts on the political front—the 101st Senator on this issue in Congress. First secret talks with IRA.

1990 Peter Brooke, British Secretary of State for Northern Ireland, declares Britain no longer has any selfish interest in Northern Ireland, either economic or strategic.

1991 The IRA fire mortar bombs into the garden of 10 Downing Street, London.

1992 One hundred pounds of Semtex exploded at the Baltic Exchange in London. Gerry Adams loses his seat in Westminster parliament to Dr. Joe Hendron of the SDLP.

1993 After many secret sessions between Hume and Sinn Féin president, Gerry Adams, they issue their first joint statement.

1994 Fragile peace is achieved. With Hume's help, American visa granted to Gerry Adams. Hume pushes Dublin and London not to miss the opportunity; ceasefire holds.

1995 John Major and John Bruton agree on outline for peace negotiations. President Clinton becomes the first US president to visit Belfast and Derry.

1996 In February, the IRA end their ceasefire. Both governments name June 10 as agreed date for all-party talks.

Index

HAMILTON DISTRICT
LIBRARIES